Th[...]gry Little Girls Guide to Moods cont'd

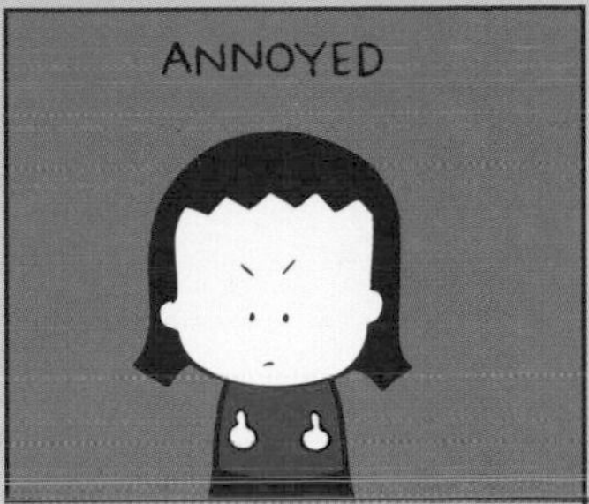
ANNOYED

Kim is also alw[...] by something. [...] her too much[...]

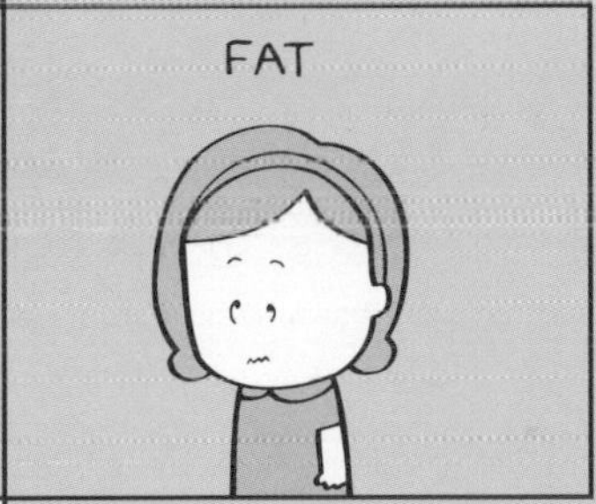
FAT

Whether she's happy or sad, she always has her favorite snacks around. It's yummy for a little while, but then she feels FAT.

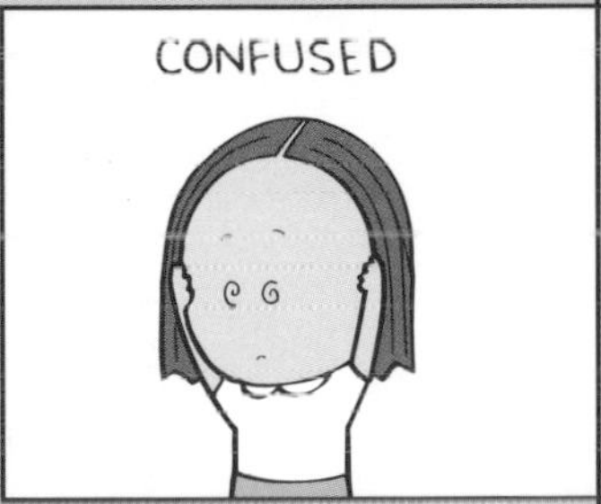
CONFUSED

Sometimes Maria gets confused by what all the "normal" people are doing.

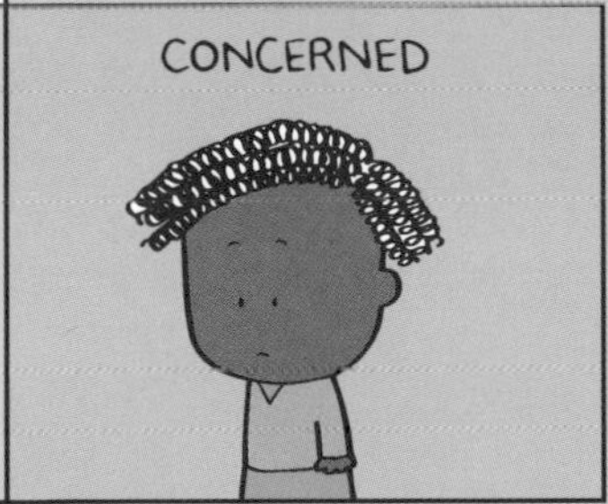
CONCERNED

Sometimes, when Wanda sees her friends unhappy she gets CONCERNED.

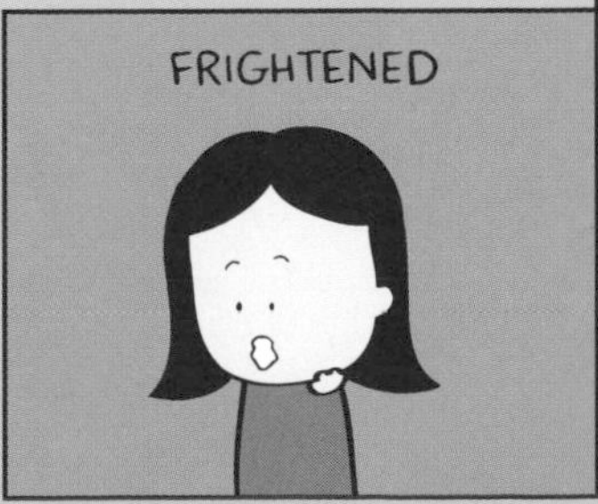
FRIGHTENED

Because Xyla sees what is terrible in everything, she also gets really FRIGHTENED!

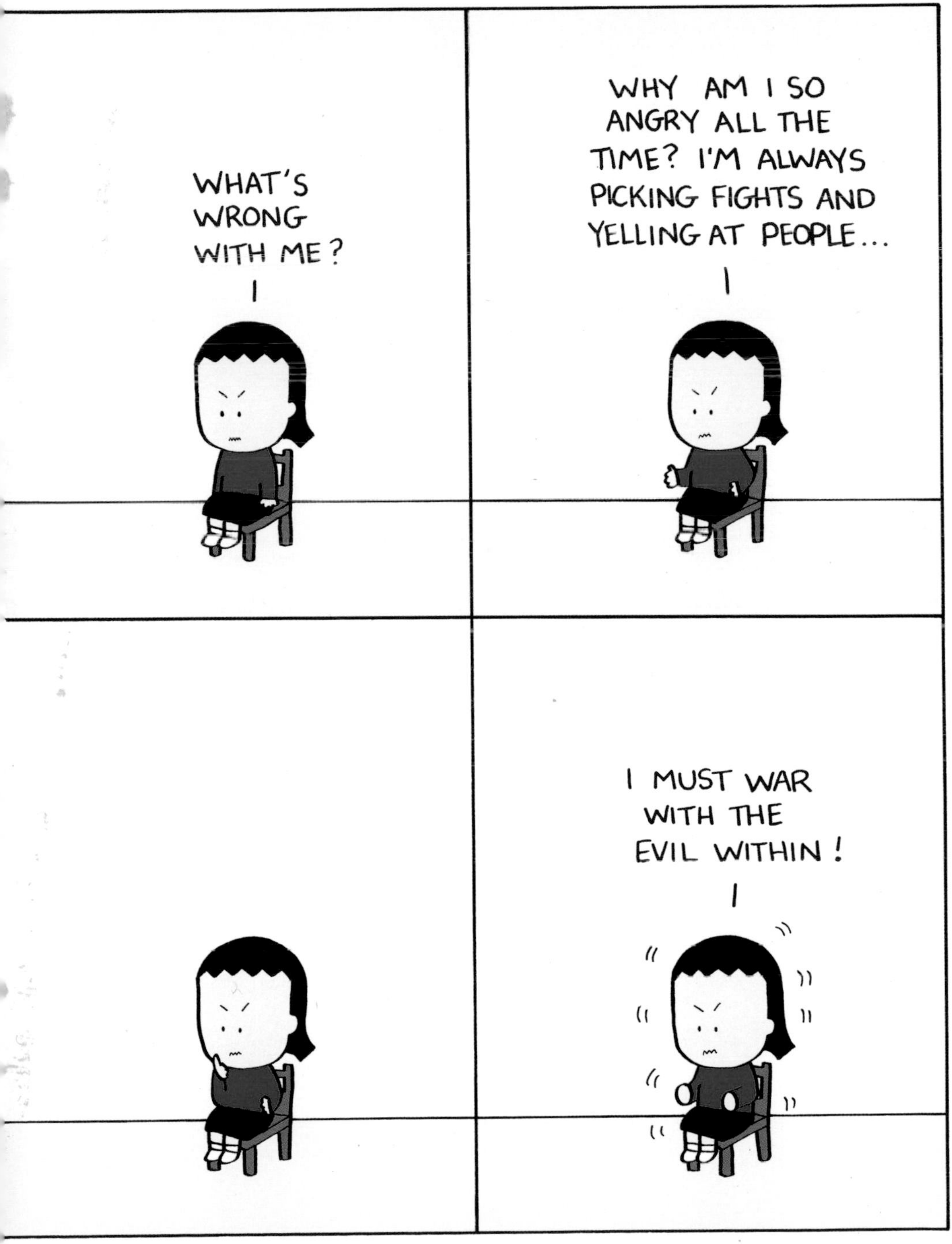

WHAT'S WRONG WITH ME?
WHY AM I SO ANGRY ALL THE TIME? I'M ALWAYS PICKING FIGHTS AND YELLING AT PEOPLE...
I MUST WAR WITH THE EVIL WITHIN!

STILL ANGRY LITTLE GIRLS

by Lela Lee

ABRAMS IMAGE
New York

Special thanks to:

My editor, Tamar Brazis;
Everyone at Harry N. Abrams, Inc., especially Vivian Cheng and Inbal Vellucci;
My legal counsel: David Rosenbaum, Amy Christensen, Jonathan Hyman, and
Jeff Van Hoosear;
My dear husband Ken and my adorable muse Neko-chan.

Editor: Tamar Brazis
Designer: Vivian Cheng
Production Manager: Kaija Markoe

Library of Congress Control Number has been applied for.
ISBN 0-8109-4915-6

Printed and bound in China
10 9 8 7 6 5 4 3 2 1

HNA
harry n. abrams, inc.
a subsidiary of La Martinière Groupe
115 West 18th Street
New York, NY 10011
www.hnabooks.com

To all the
"angry little girls"
(and boys) out
there who made
Angry Little Girls
a great success,
<u>Thank you</u>
from the bottom of
my heart.

Stay Angry!

♥, Lela

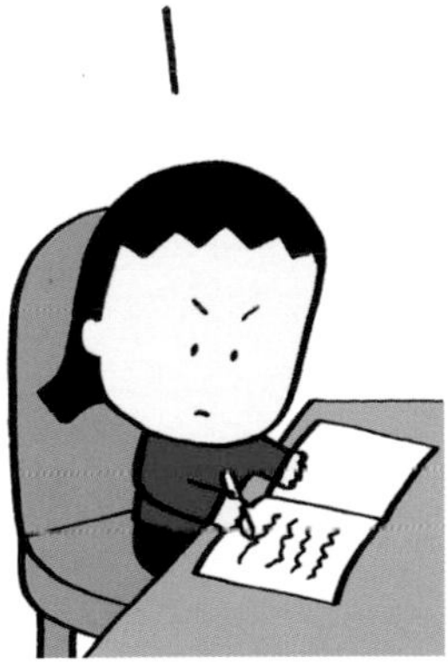

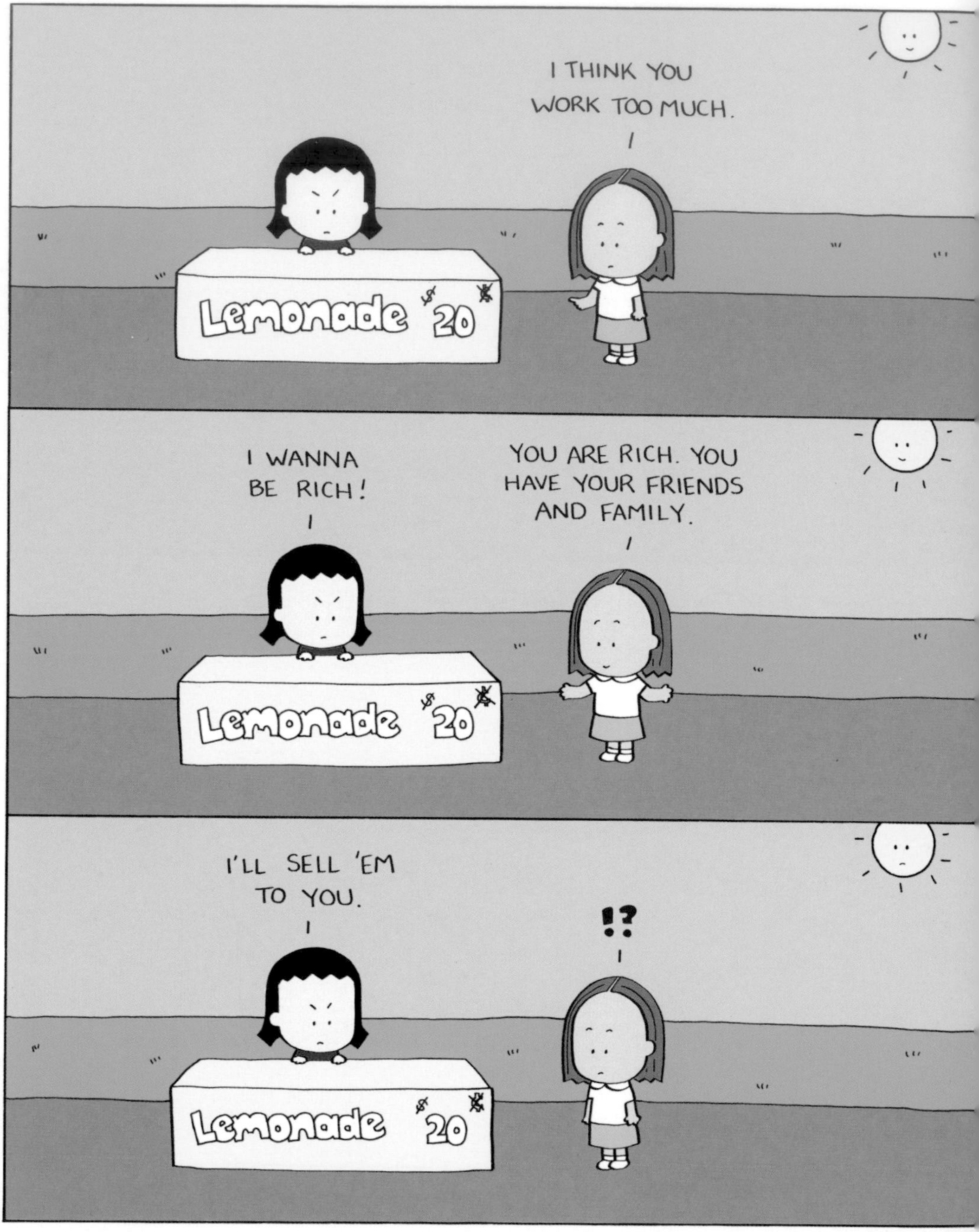
I THINK YOU WORK TOO MUCH.
Lemonade $ 20 ¢
I WANNA BE RICH!
YOU ARE RICH. YOU HAVE YOUR FRIENDS AND FAMILY.
Lemonade $ 20 ¢
I'LL SELL 'EM TO YOU.
!?
Lemonade $ 20 ¢

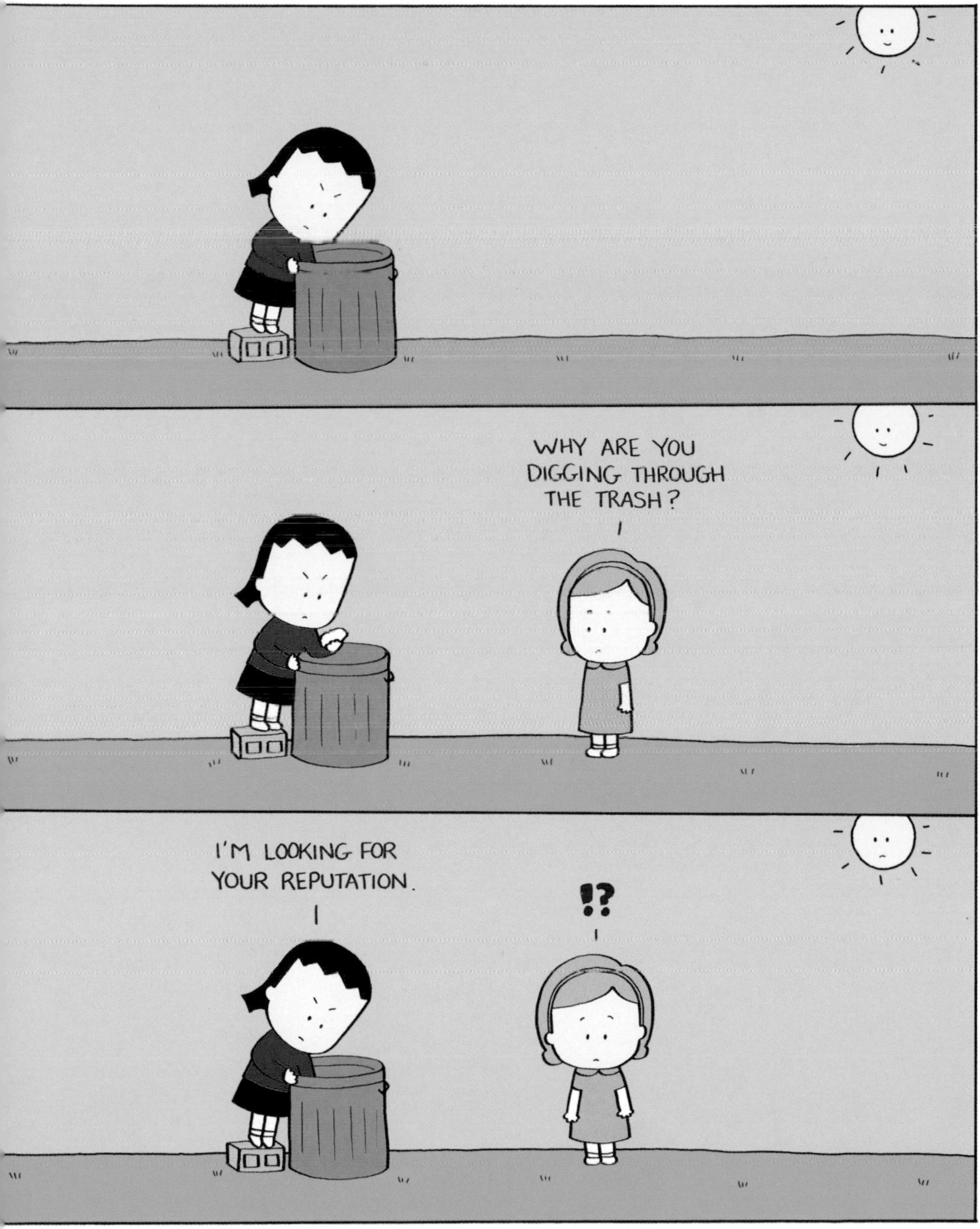
WHY ARE YOU DIGGING THROUGH THE TRASH?
I'M LOOKING FOR YOUR REPUTATION.
!?

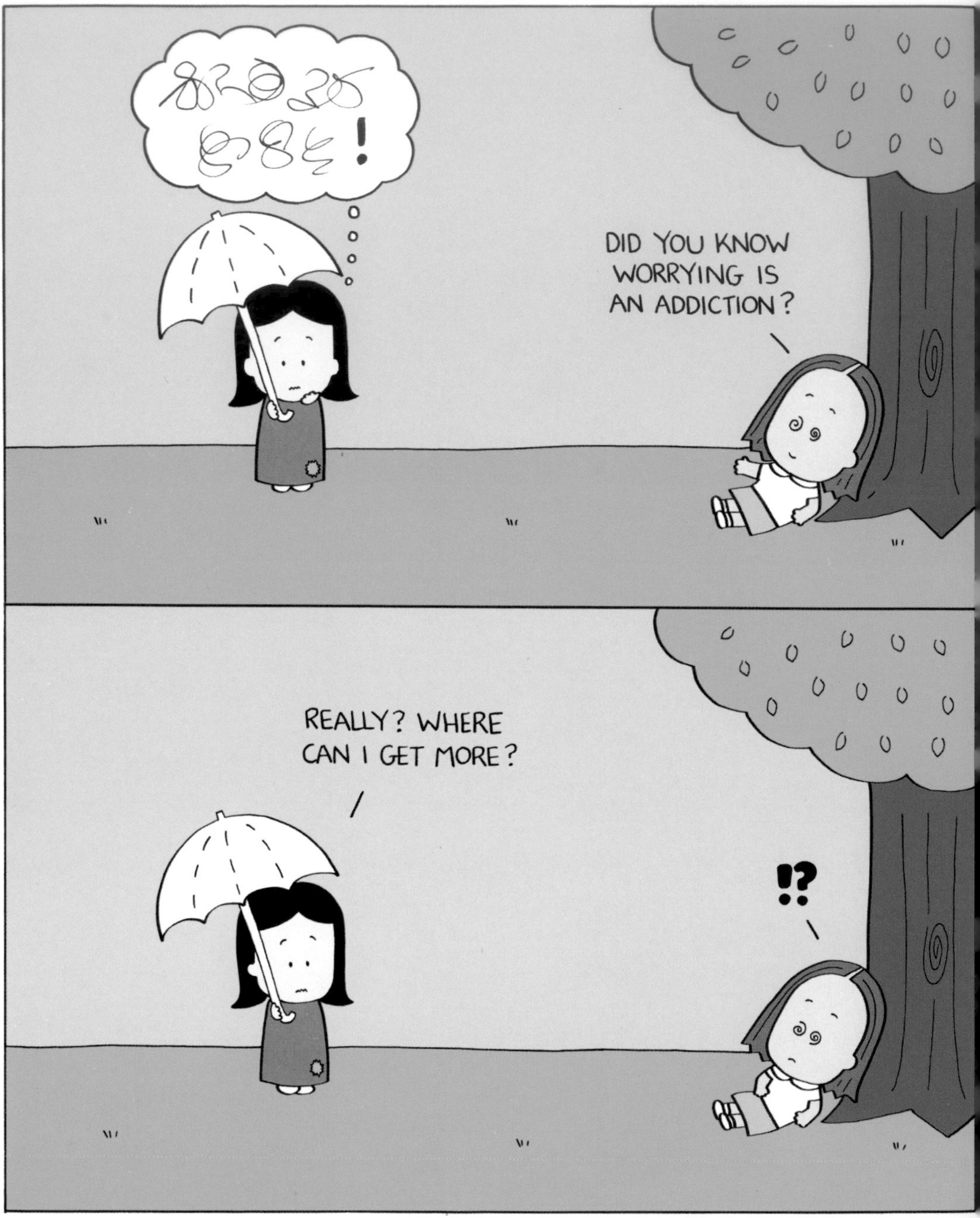
DID YOU KNOW WORRYING IS AN ADDICTION?
REALLY? WHERE CAN I GET MORE?
!?

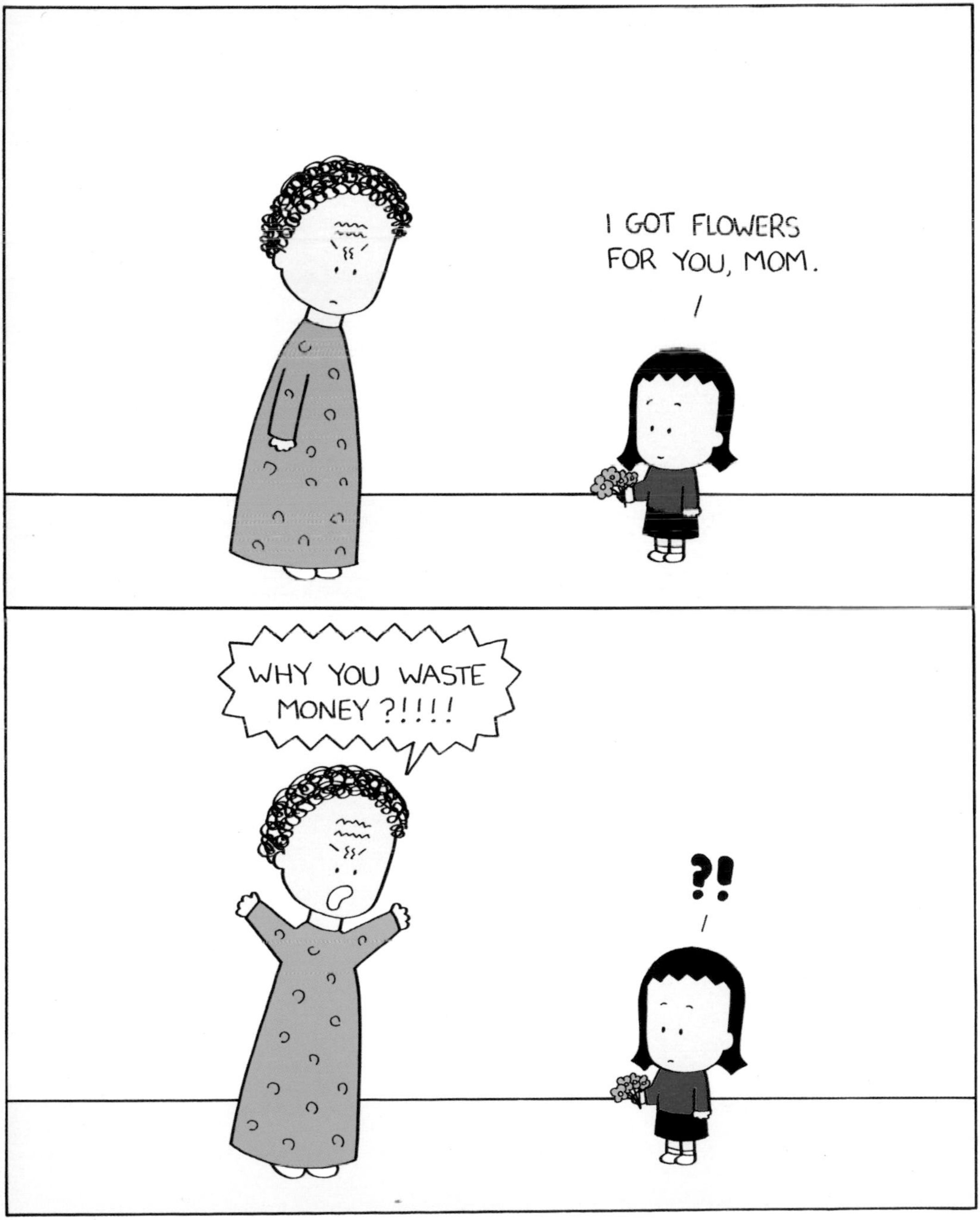
I GOT FLOWERS FOR YOU, MOM.
WHY YOU WASTE MONEY ?!!!!
?!

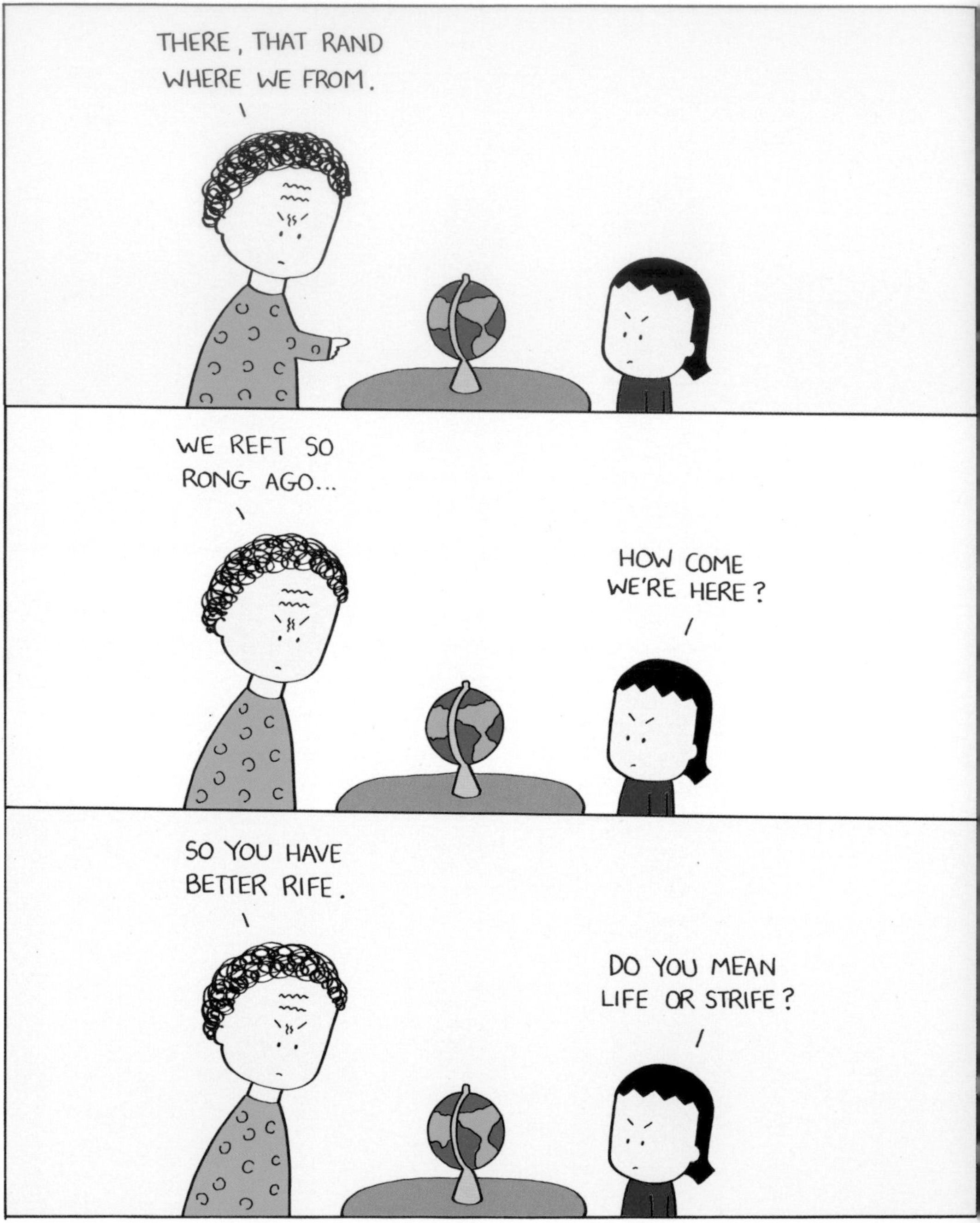
THERE, THAT RAND WHERE WE FROM.
WE REFT SO RONG AGO...
HOW COME WE'RE HERE?
SO YOU HAVE BETTER RIFE.
DO YOU MEAN LIFE OR STRIFE?

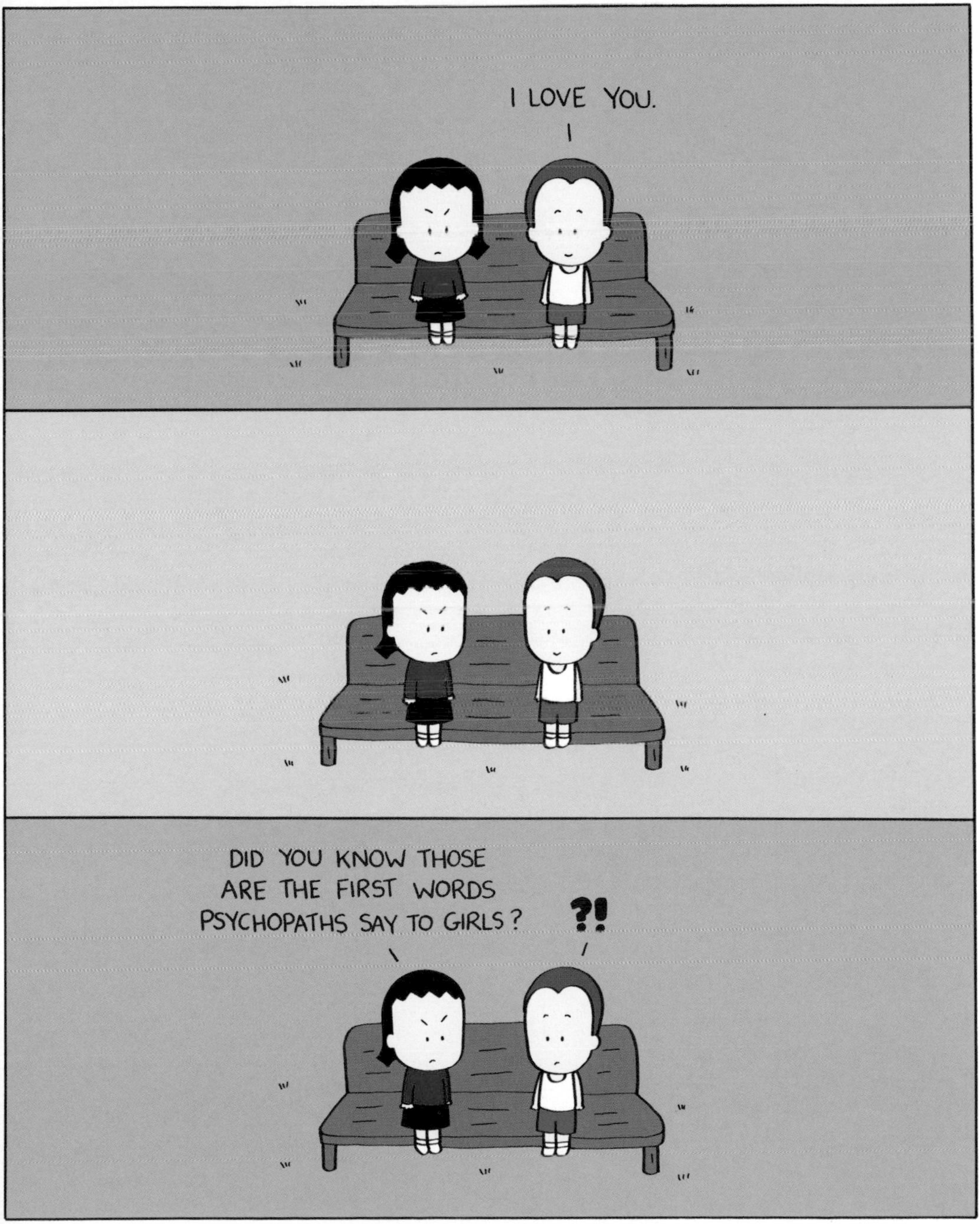
I LOVE YOU.
DID YOU KNOW THOSE ARE THE FIRST WORDS PSYCHOPATHS SAY TO GIRLS?
?!

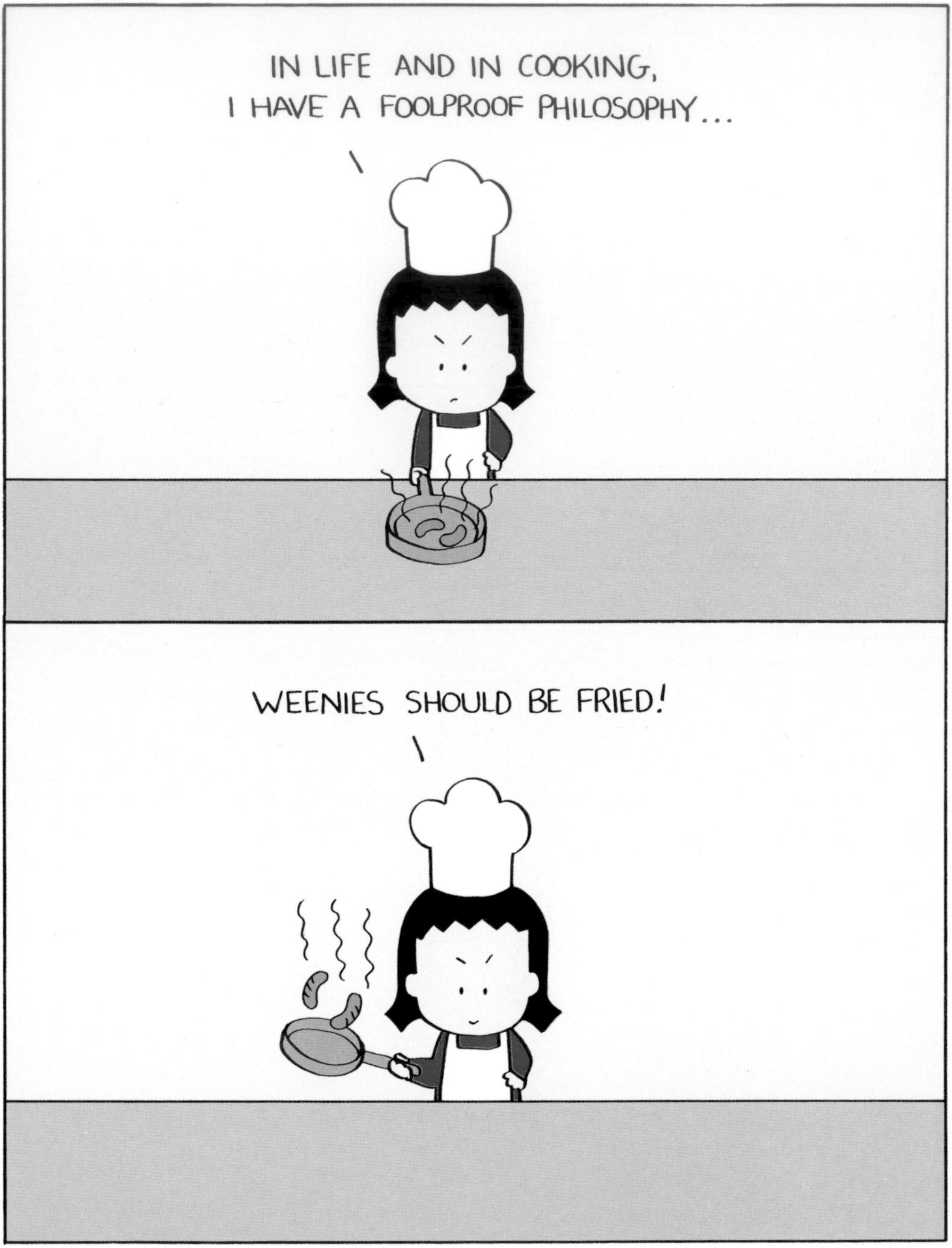
IN LIFE AND IN COOKING,
I HAVE A FOOLPROOF PHILOSOPHY...
WEENIES SHOULD BE FRIED!

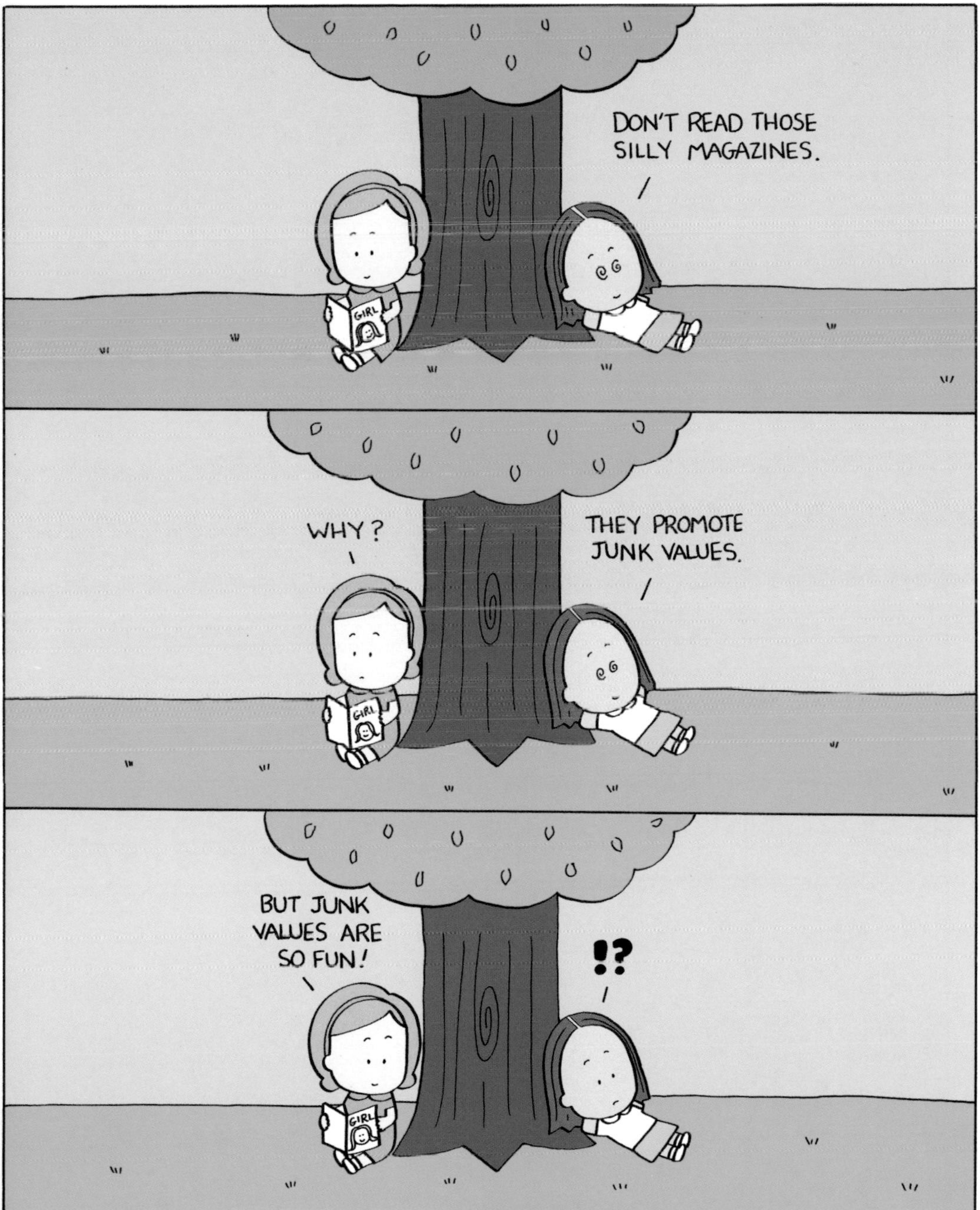
DON'T READ THOSE SILLY MAGAZINES.
GIRL
WHY?
THEY PROMOTE JUNK VALUES.
GIRL
BUT JUNK VALUES ARE SO FUN!
!?
GIRL

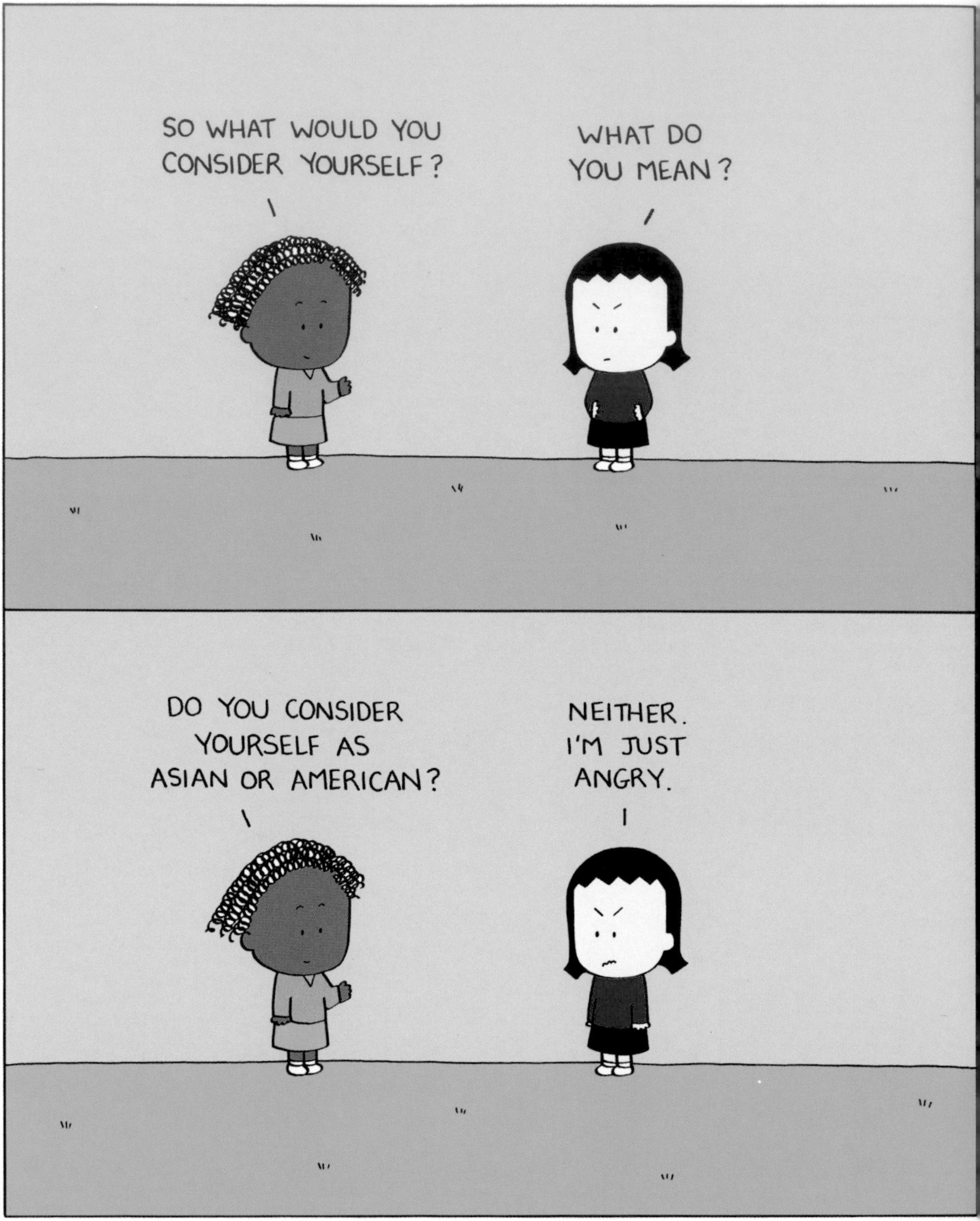
SO WHAT WOULD YOU CONSIDER YOURSELF?
WHAT DO YOU MEAN?
DO YOU CONSIDER YOURSELF AS ASIAN OR AMERICAN?
NEITHER. I'M JUST ANGRY.

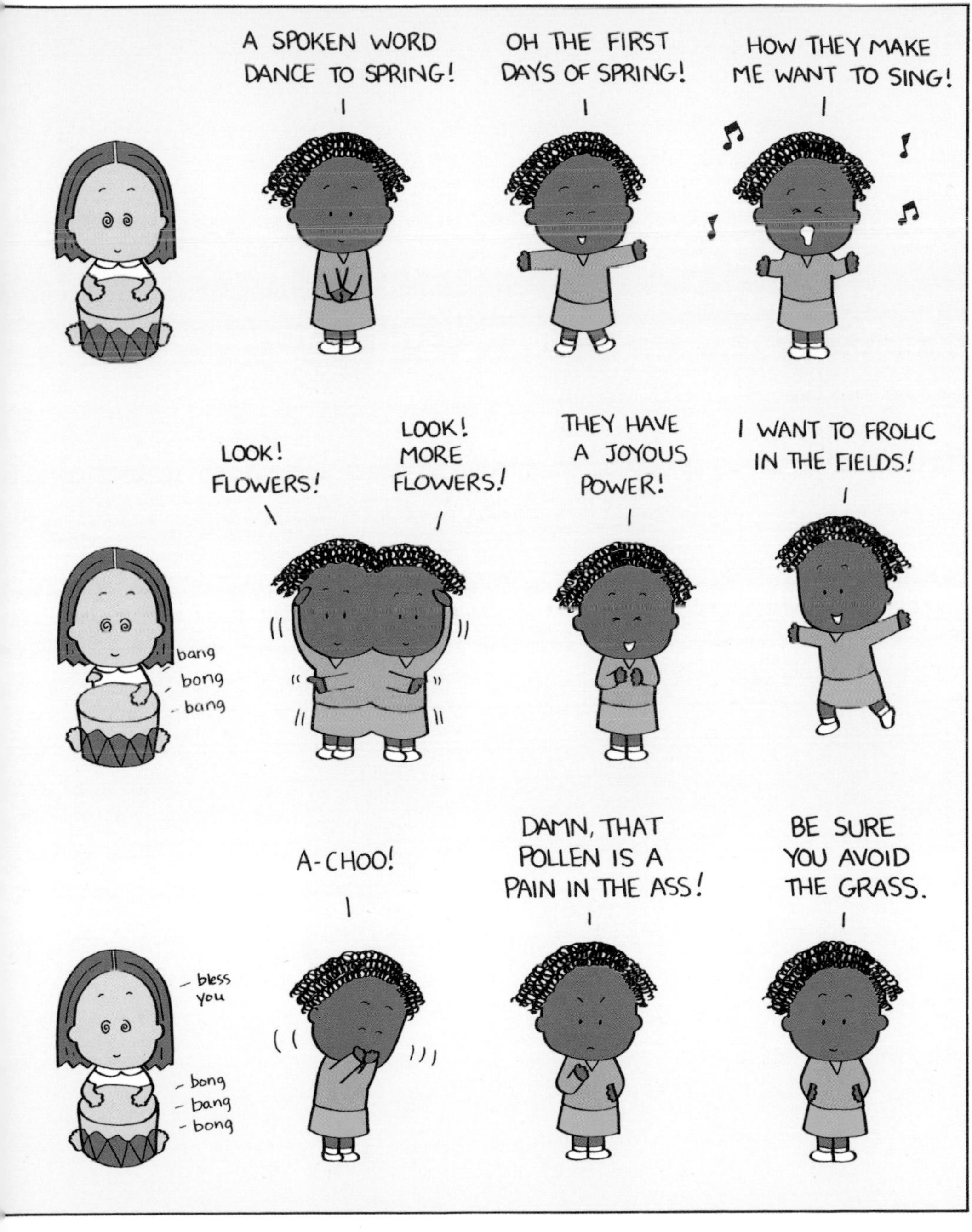
A SPOKEN WORD DANCE TO SPRING!
OH THE FIRST DAYS OF SPRING!
HOW THEY MAKE ME WANT TO SING!
LOOK! FLOWERS!
LOOK! MORE FLOWERS!
THEY HAVE A JOYOUS POWER!
I WANT TO FROLIC IN THE FIELDS!
bang
bong
bang
A-CHOO!
DAMN, THAT POLLEN IS A PAIN IN THE ASS!
BE SURE YOU AVOID THE GRASS.
bless you
bong
bang
bong

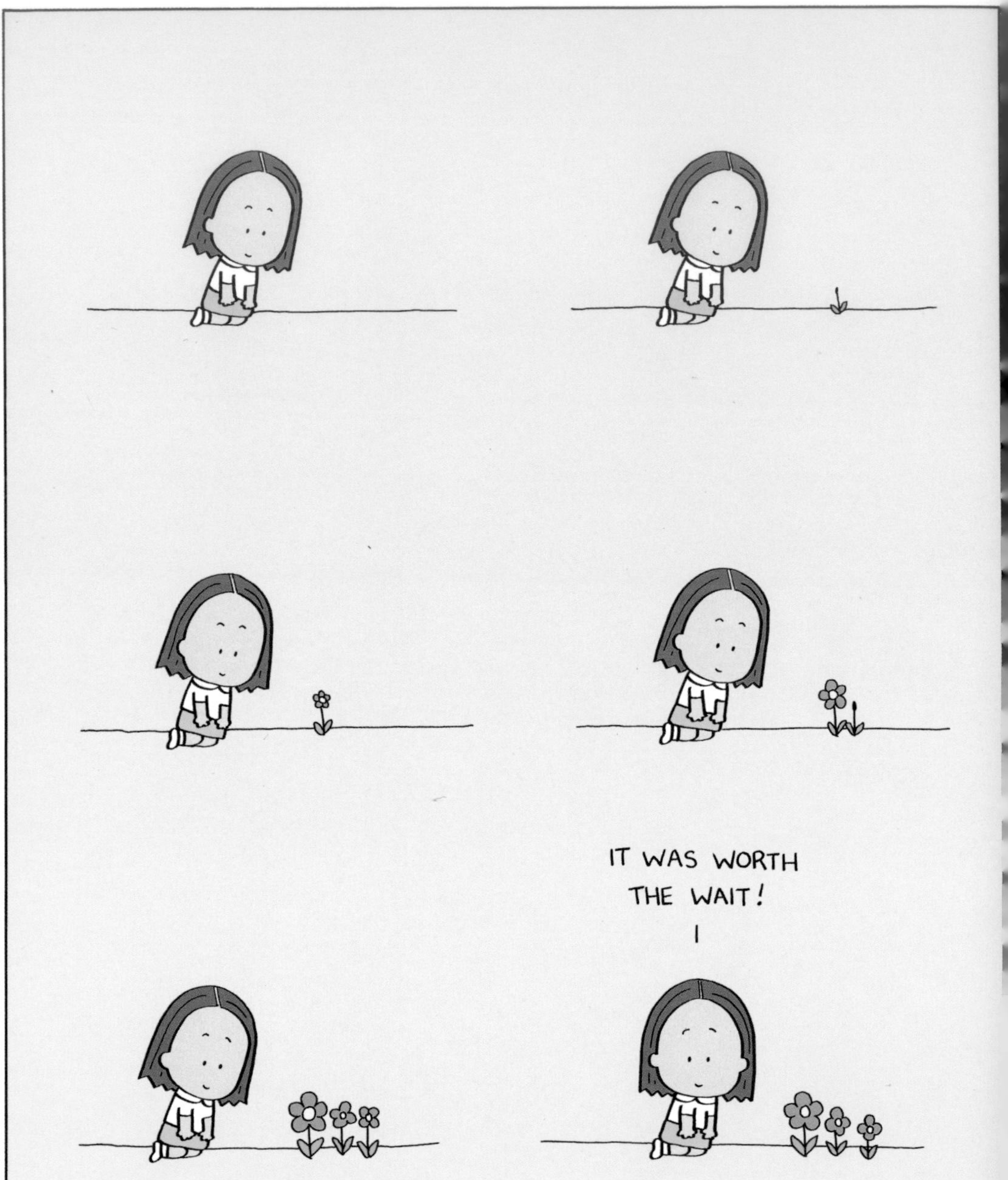
IT WAS WORTH THE WAIT!

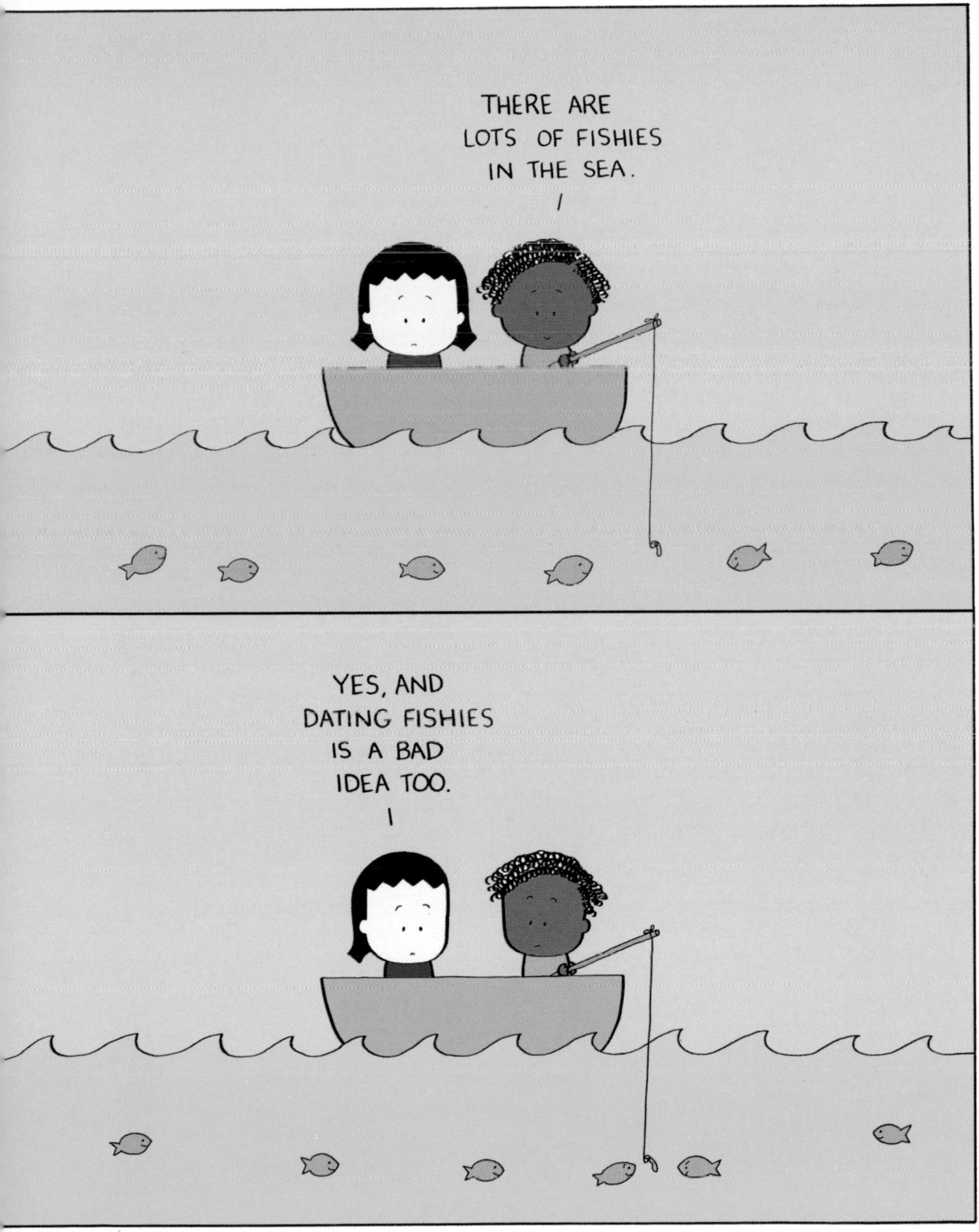
THERE ARE LOTS OF FISHIES IN THE SEA.
YES, AND DATING FISHIES IS A BAD IDEA TOO.

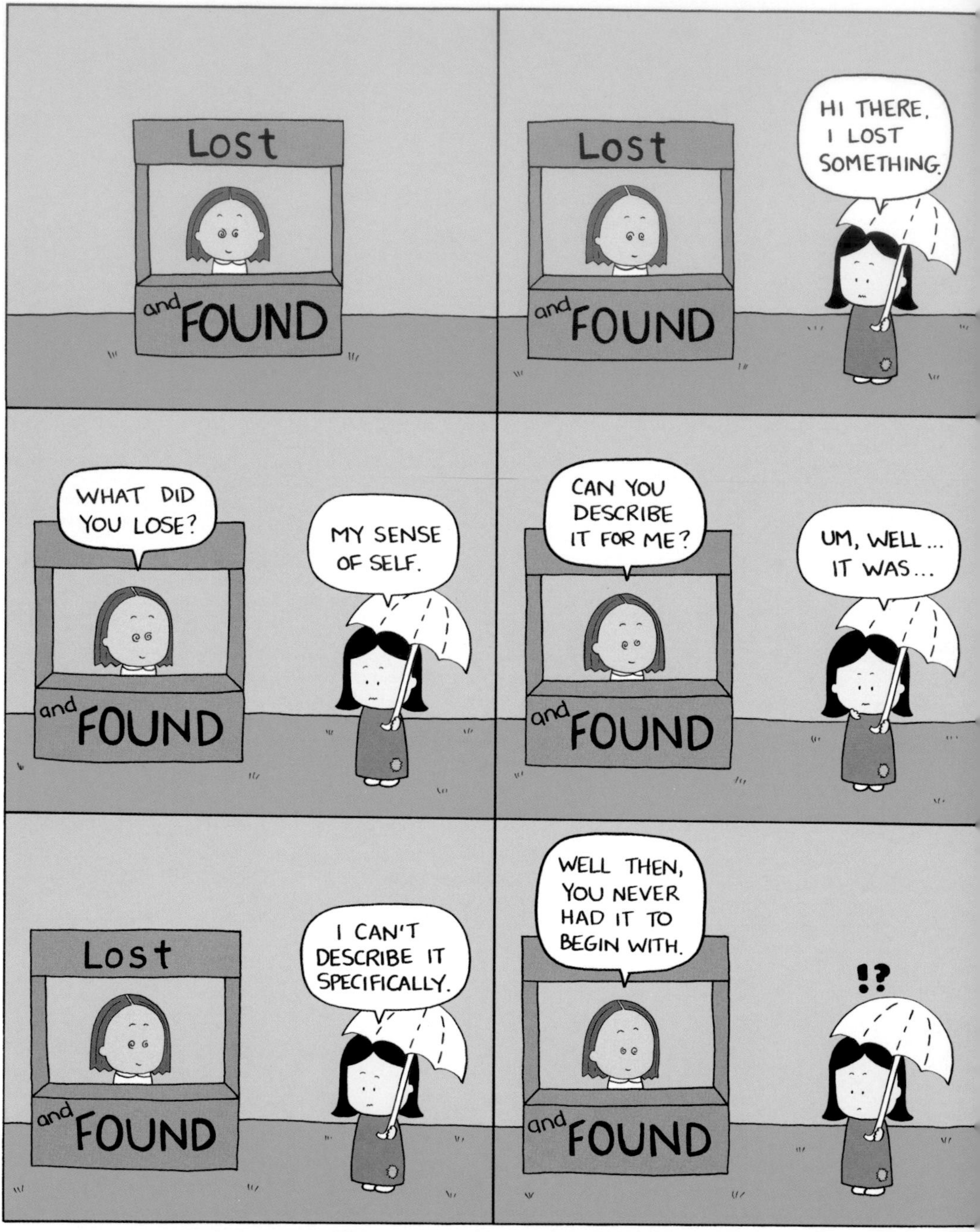
Lost
and FOUND
Lost
and FOUND
HI THERE, I LOST SOMETHING.
WHAT DID YOU LOSE?
and FOUND
MY SENSE OF SELF.
CAN YOU DESCRIBE IT FOR ME?
and FOUND
UM, WELL... IT WAS...
Lost
and FOUND
I CAN'T DESCRIBE IT SPECIFICALLY.
WELL THEN, YOU NEVER HAD IT TO BEGIN WITH.
and FOUND
!?

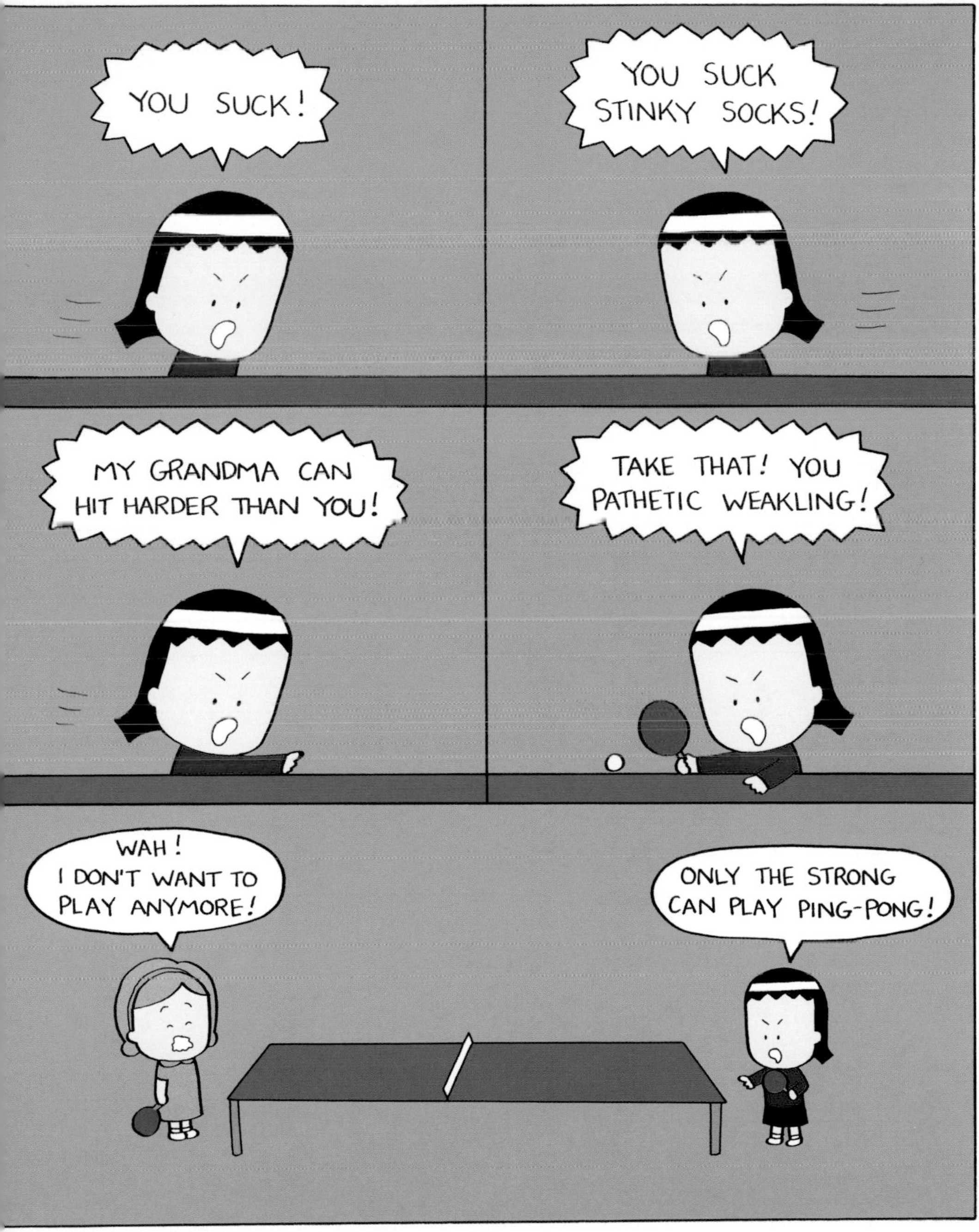
YOU SUCK!
YOU SUCK STINKY SOCKS!
MY GRANDMA CAN HIT HARDER THAN YOU!
TAKE THAT! YOU PATHETIC WEAKLING!
WAH! I DON'T WANT TO PLAY ANYMORE!
ONLY THE STRONG CAN PLAY PING-PONG!

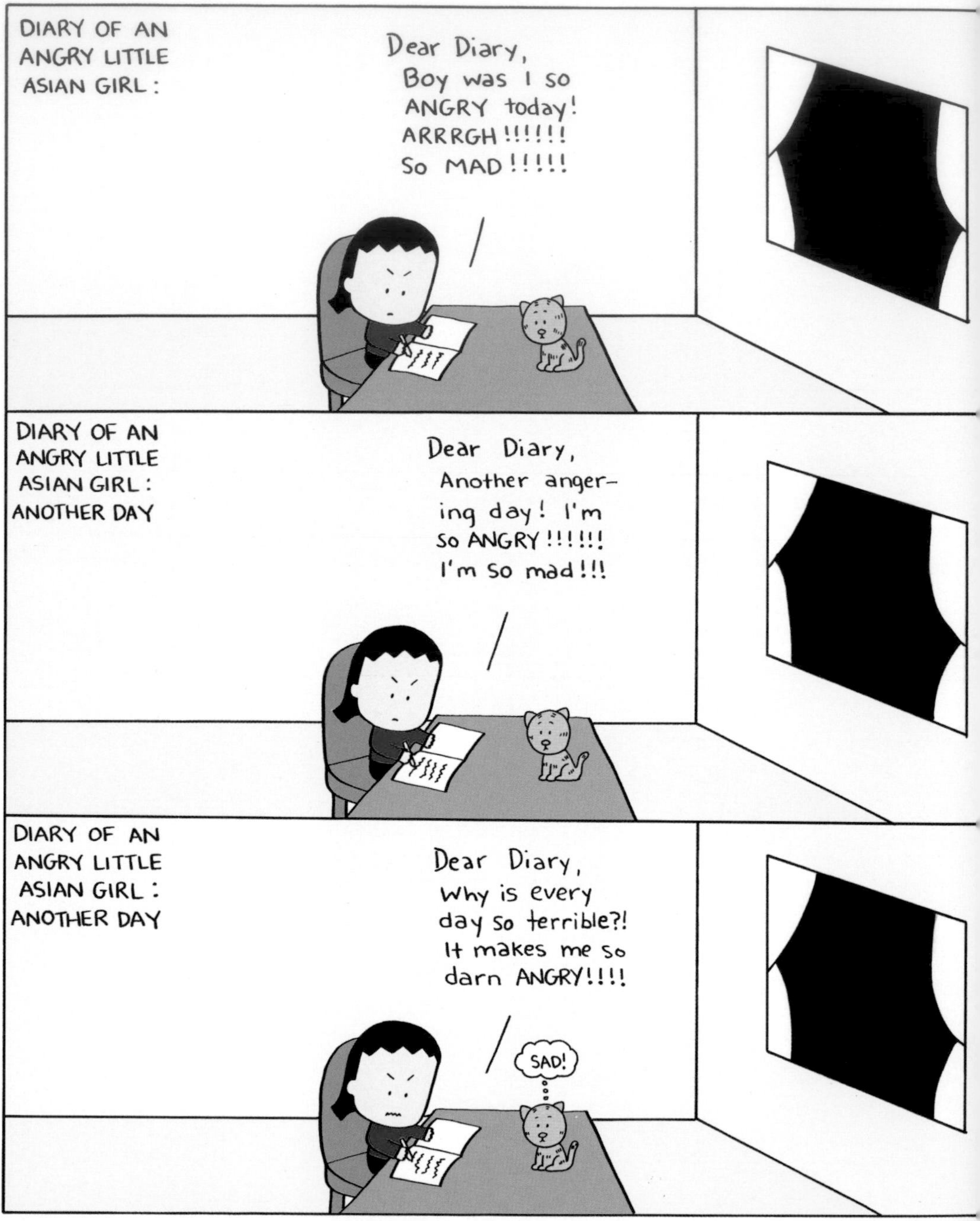
DIARY OF AN ANGRY LITTLE ASIAN GIRL:
Dear Diary, Boy was I so ANGRY today! ARRRGH!!!!!! So MAD!!!!!
DIARY OF AN ANGRY LITTLE ASIAN GIRL: ANOTHER DAY
Dear Diary, Another angering day! I'm so ANGRY!!!!!! I'm so mad!!!
DIARY OF AN ANGRY LITTLE ASIAN GIRL: ANOTHER DAY
Dear Diary, Why is every day so terrible?! It makes me so darn ANGRY!!!!
SAD!

ARE YOU
"AUTHENTIC"?
I

ARE YOU
"ORIGINAL"?
I

ARE YOU
"REAL"?

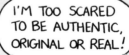

I'M TOO SCARED TO BE AUTHENTIC, ORIGINAL OR REAL!

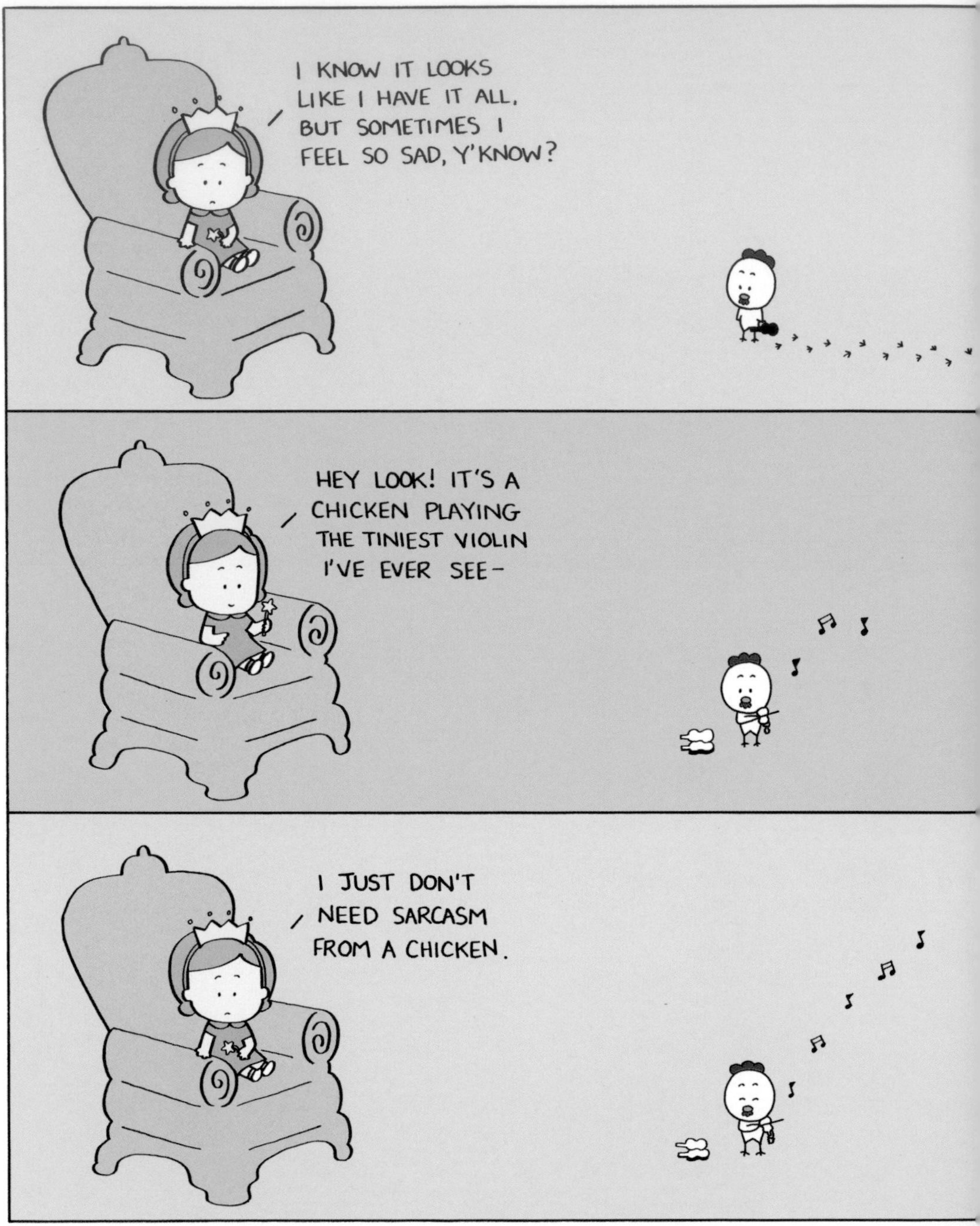
I KNOW IT LOOKS LIKE I HAVE IT ALL, BUT SOMETIMES I FEEL SO SAD, Y'KNOW?
HEY LOOK! IT'S A CHICKEN PLAYING THE TINIEST VIOLIN I'VE EVER SEE-
I JUST DON'T NEED SARCASM FROM A CHICKEN.

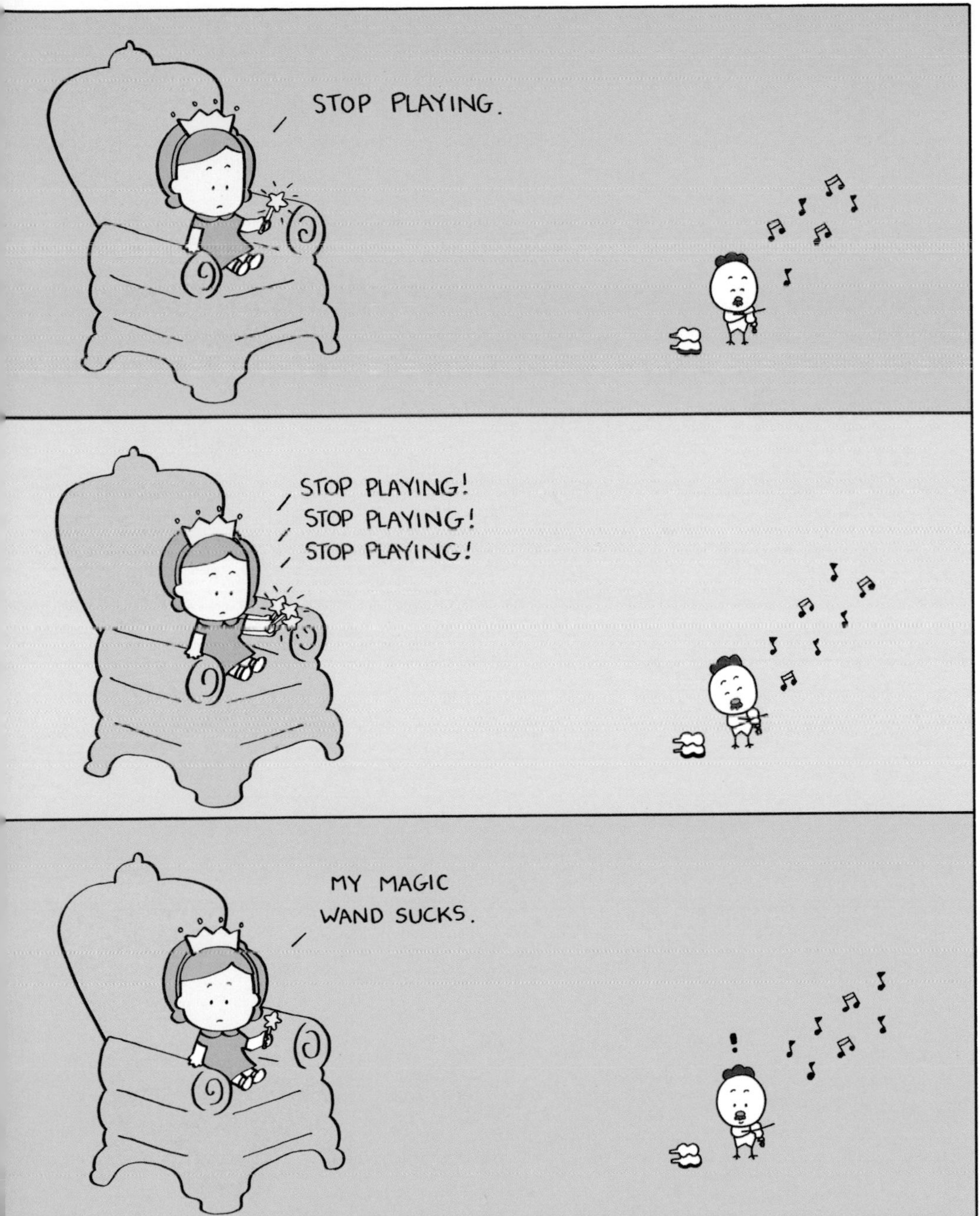
STOP PLAYING.
STOP PLAYING! STOP PLAYING! STOP PLAYING!
MY MAGIC WAND SUCKS.

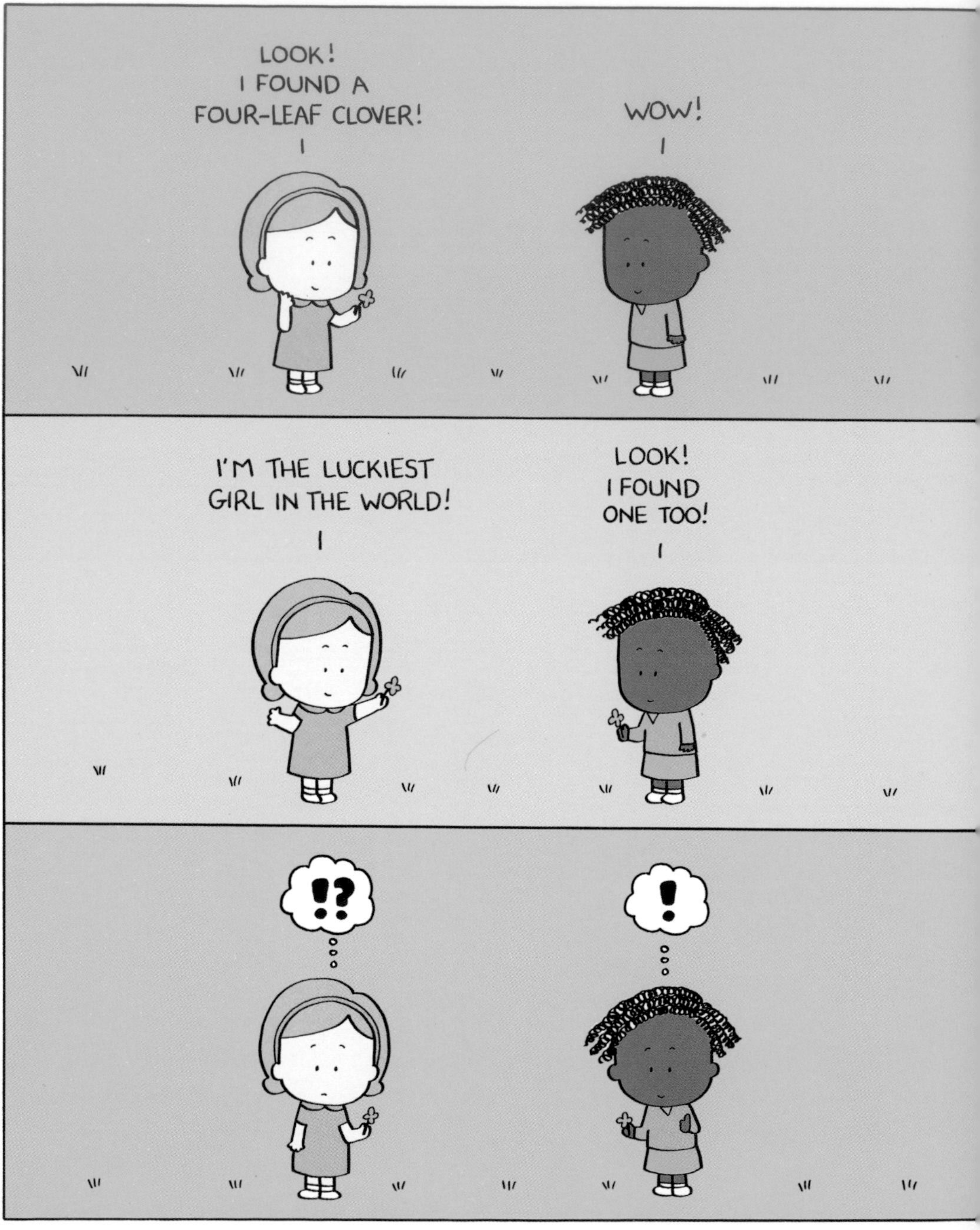
LOOK! I FOUND A FOUR-LEAF CLOVER!
WOW!
I'M THE LUCKIEST GIRL IN THE WORLD!
LOOK! I FOUND ONE TOO!
!?
!

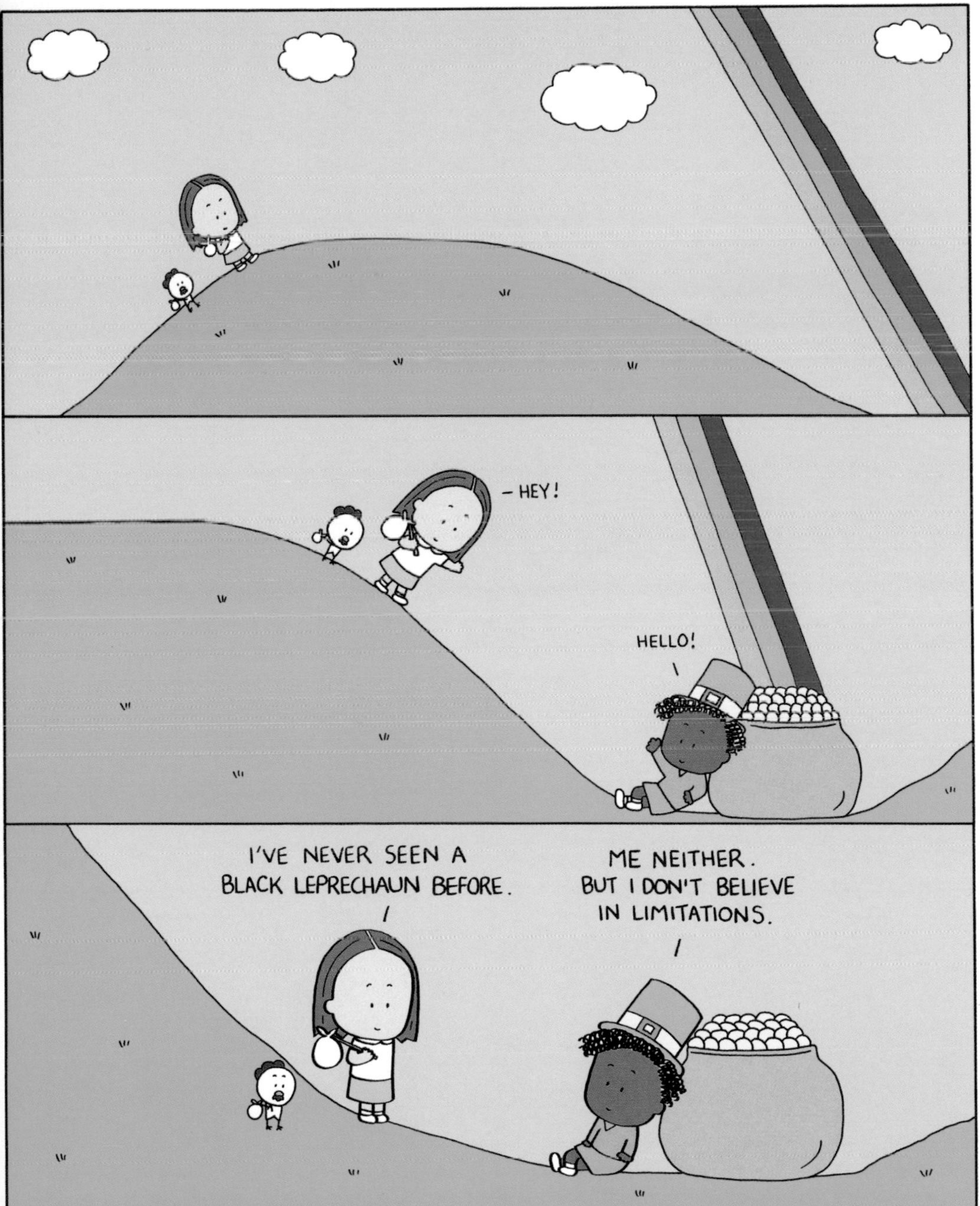
- HEY!
HELLO!
I'VE NEVER SEEN A BLACK LEPRECHAUN BEFORE.
ME NEITHER. BUT I DON'T BELIEVE IN LIMITATIONS.

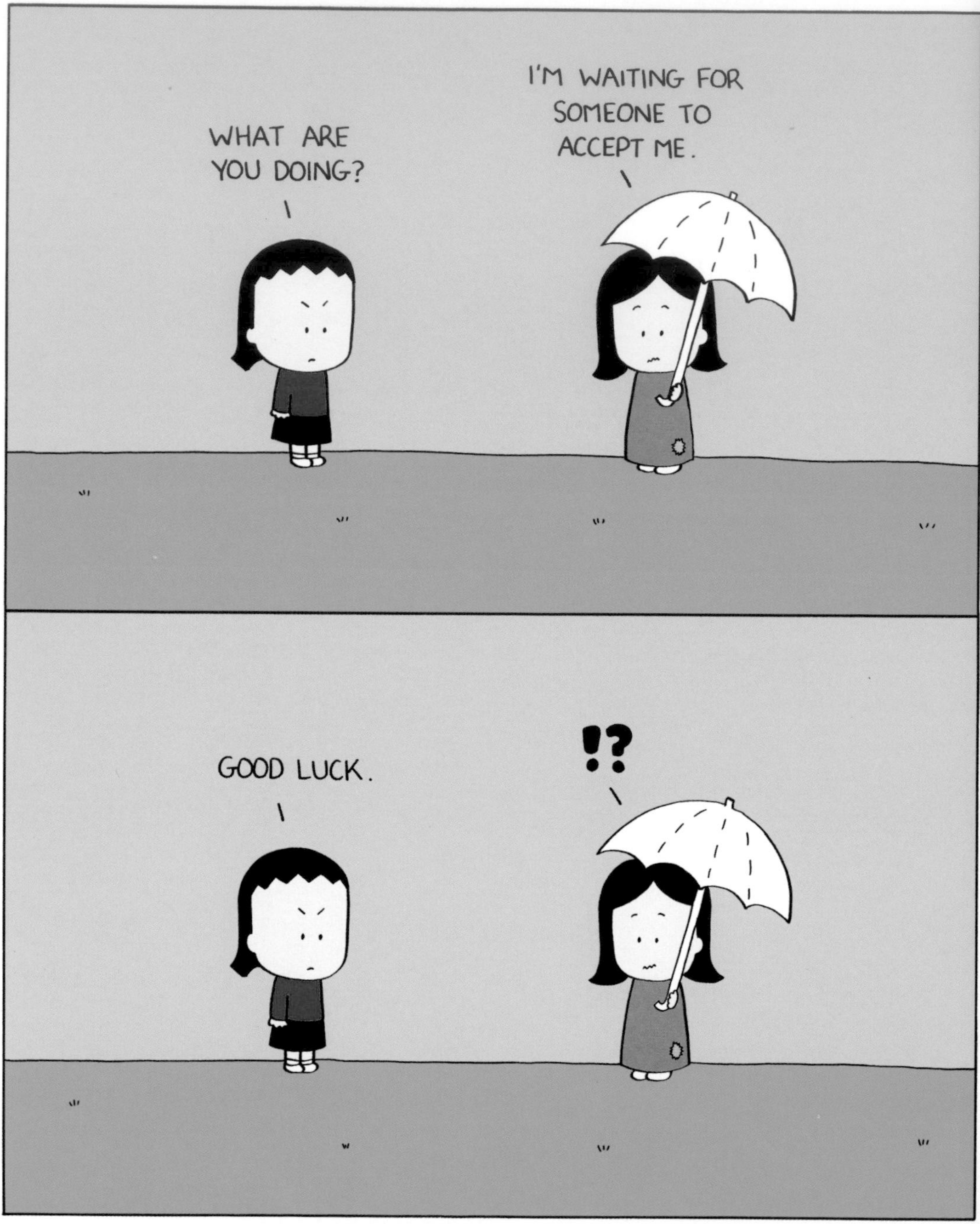
WHAT ARE YOU DOING?
I'M WAITING FOR SOMEONE TO ACCEPT ME.
GOOD LUCK.
!?

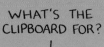

WHAT'S THE
CLIPBOARD FOR?

I'M KEEPING
TRACK.

KEEPING TRACK
OF WHAT?

OF HOW MANY
TIMES YOU
ANNOY ME.

!?

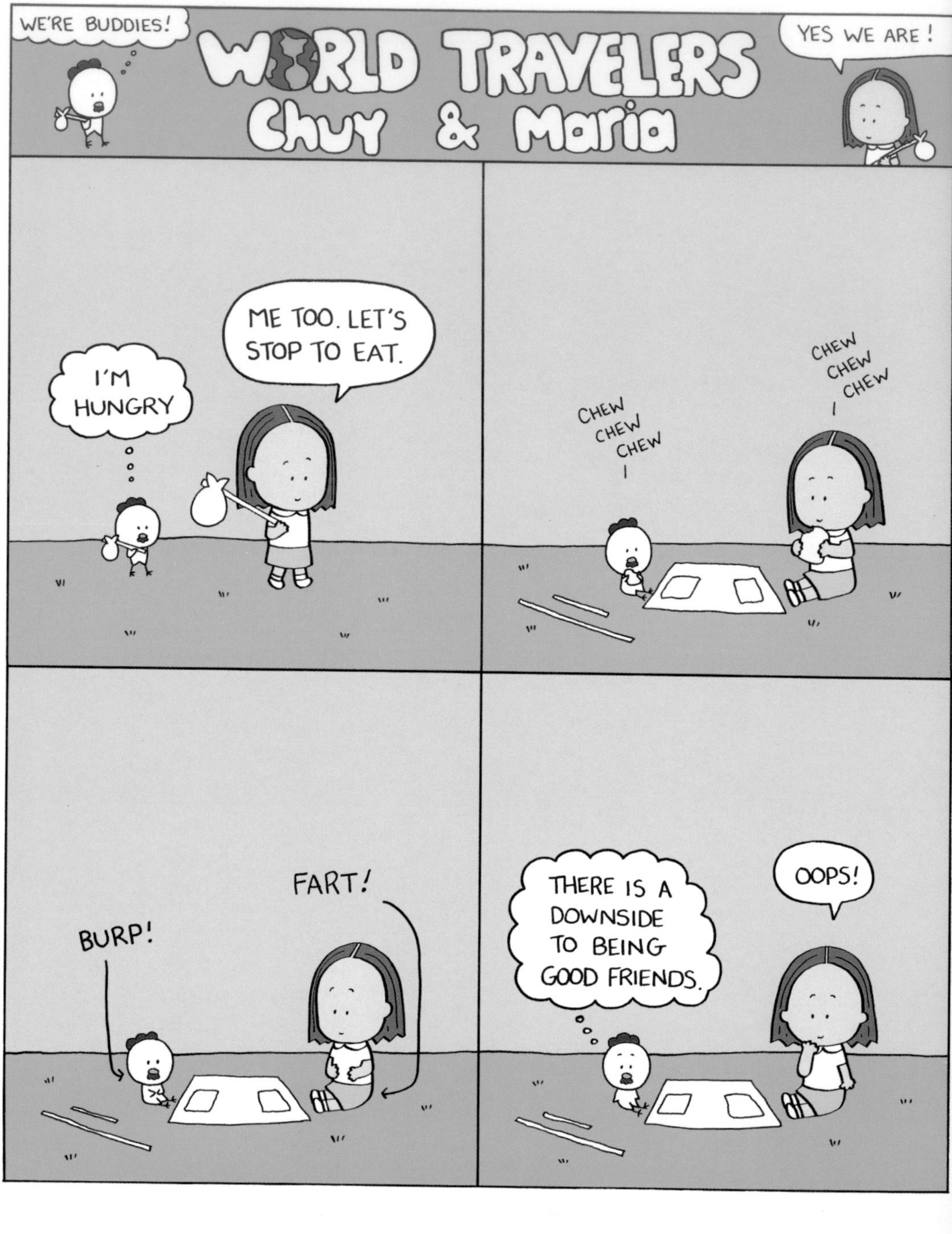
WE'RE BUDDIES!
WORLD TRAVELERS
Chuy & Maria
YES WE ARE!
I'M HUNGRY
ME TOO. LET'S STOP TO EAT.
CHEW CHEW CHEW
CHEW CHEW CHEW
BURP!
FART!
THERE IS A DOWNSIDE TO BEING GOOD FRIENDS.
OOPS!

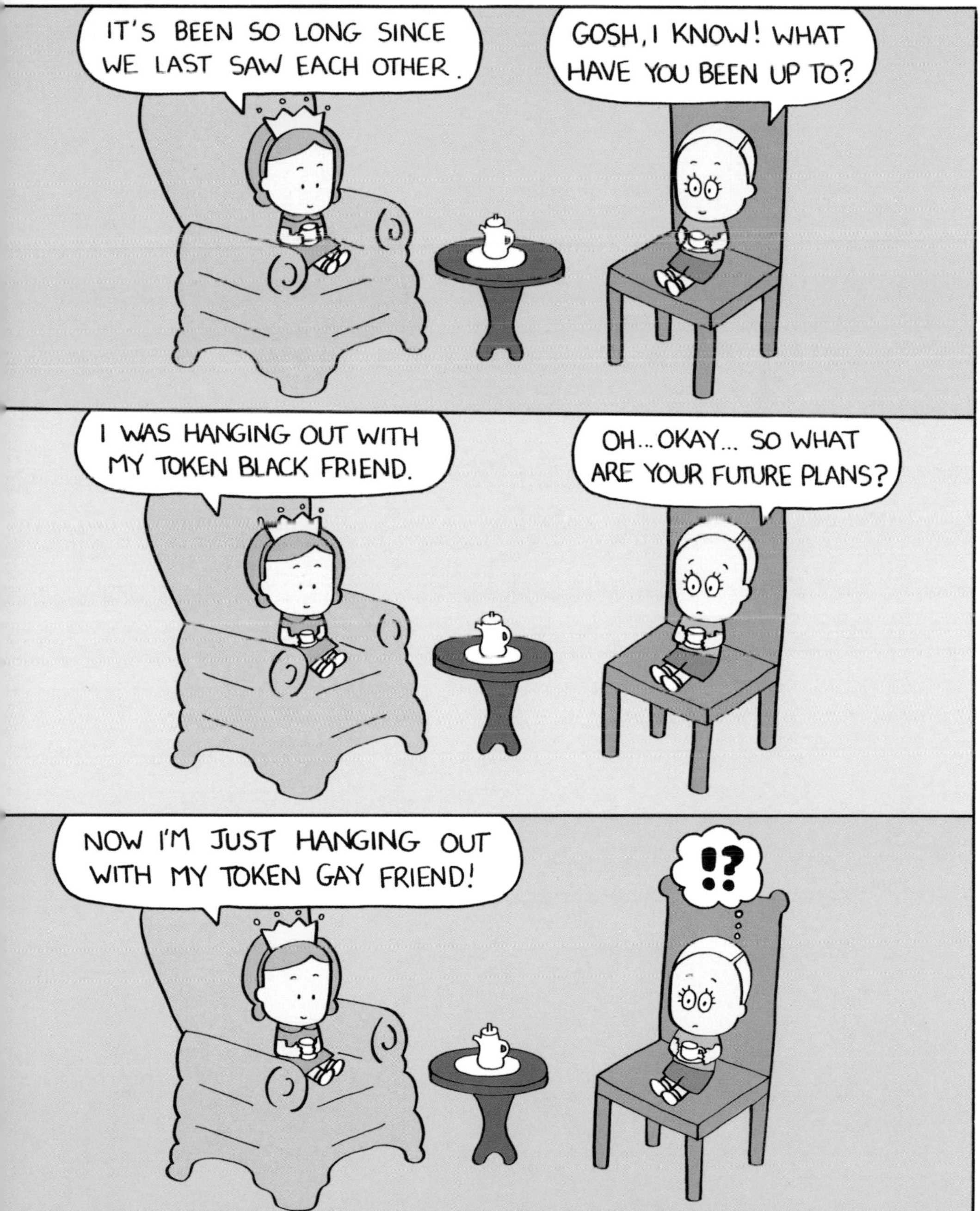
IT'S BEEN SO LONG SINCE WE LAST SAW EACH OTHER.
GOSH, I KNOW! WHAT HAVE YOU BEEN UP TO?
I WAS HANGING OUT WITH MY TOKEN BLACK FRIEND.
OH... OKAY... SO WHAT ARE YOUR FUTURE PLANS?
NOW I'M JUST HANGING OUT WITH MY TOKEN GAY FRIEND!
!?

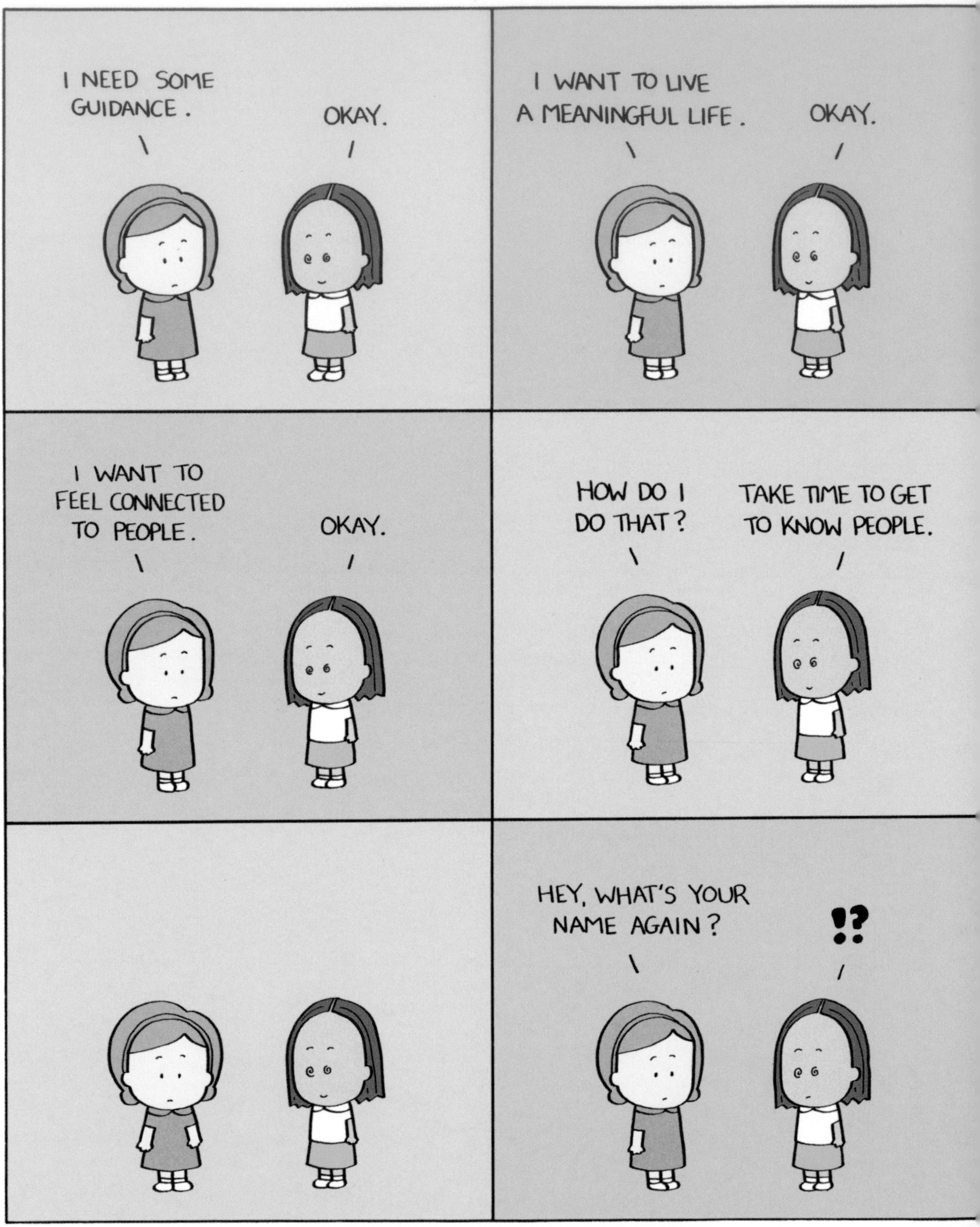
I NEED SOME GUIDANCE.
OKAY.
I WANT TO LIVE A MEANINGFUL LIFE.
OKAY.
I WANT TO FEEL CONNECTED TO PEOPLE.
OKAY.
HOW DO I DO THAT?
TAKE TIME TO GET TO KNOW PEOPLE.
HEY, WHAT'S YOUR NAME AGAIN?
!?

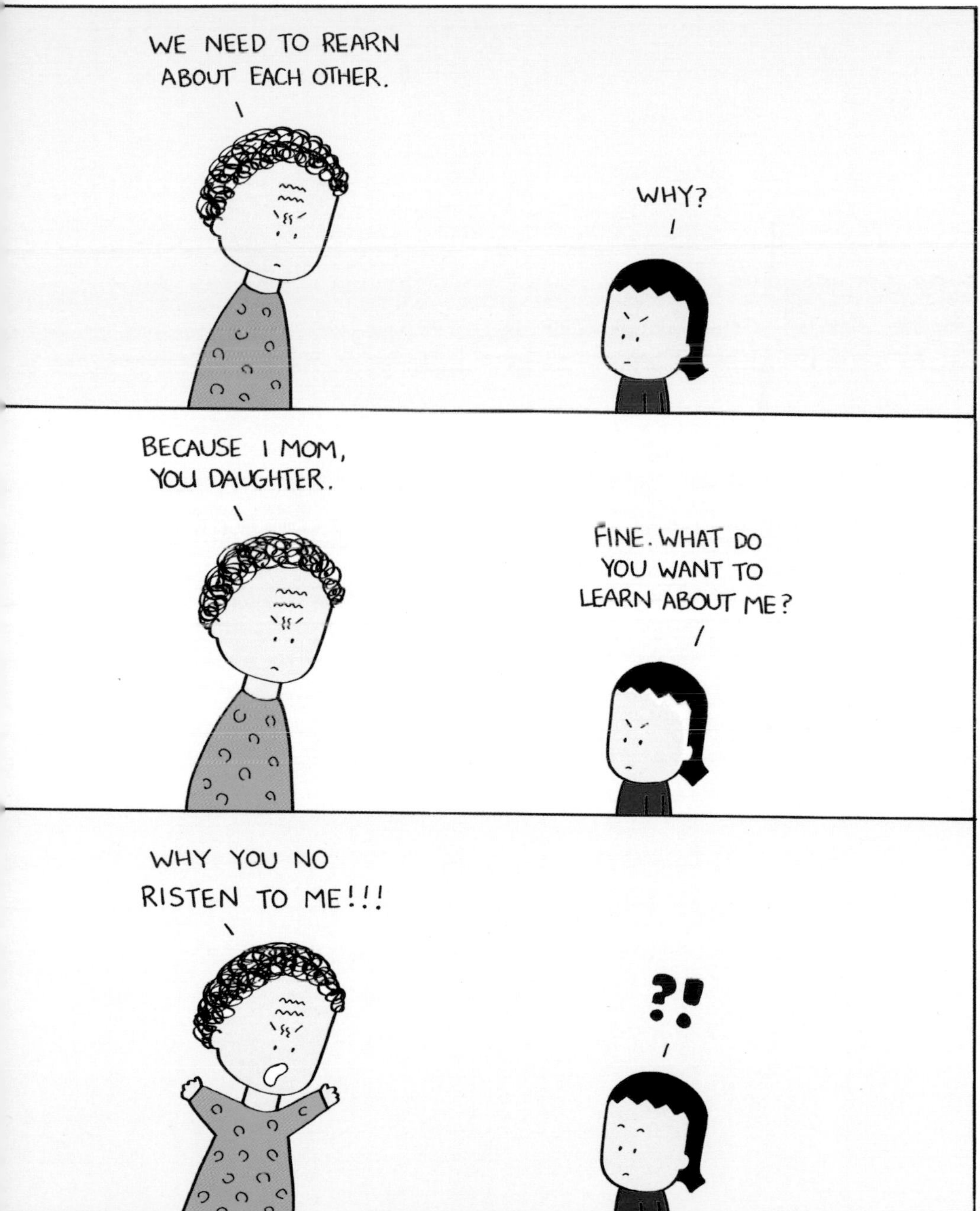
WE NEED TO REARN ABOUT EACH OTHER.
WHY?
BECAUSE I MOM, YOU DAUGHTER.
FINE. WHAT DO YOU WANT TO LEARN ABOUT ME?
WHY YOU NO RISTEN TO ME!!!
?!

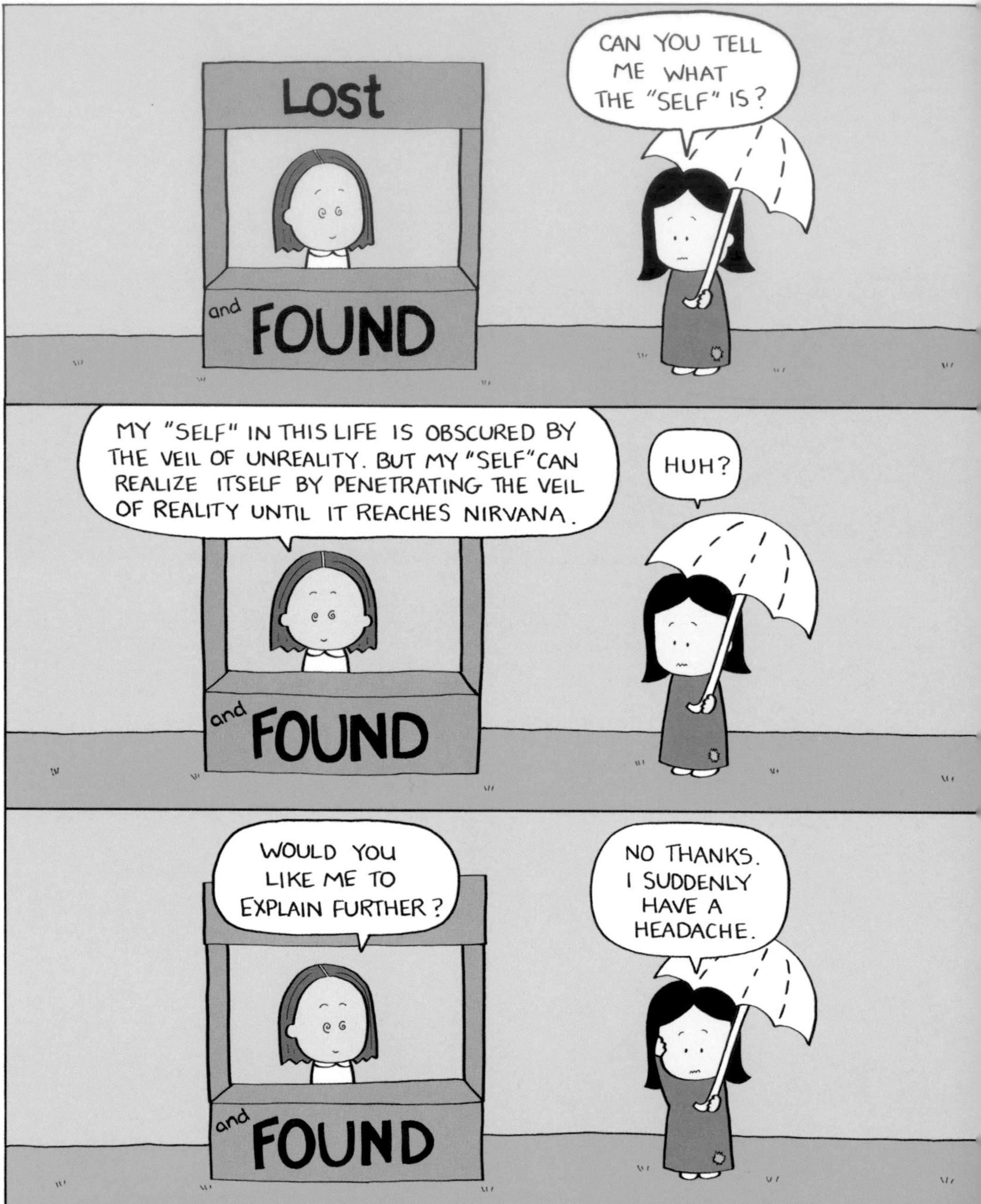
Lost
and FOUND
CAN YOU TELL ME WHAT THE "SELF" IS?
MY "SELF" IN THIS LIFE IS OBSCURED BY THE VEIL OF UNREALITY. BUT MY "SELF" CAN REALIZE ITSELF BY PENETRATING THE VEIL OF REALITY UNTIL IT REACHES NIRVANA.
HUH?
and FOUND
WOULD YOU LIKE ME TO EXPLAIN FURTHER?
NO THANKS. I SUDDENLY HAVE A HEADACHE.
and FOUND

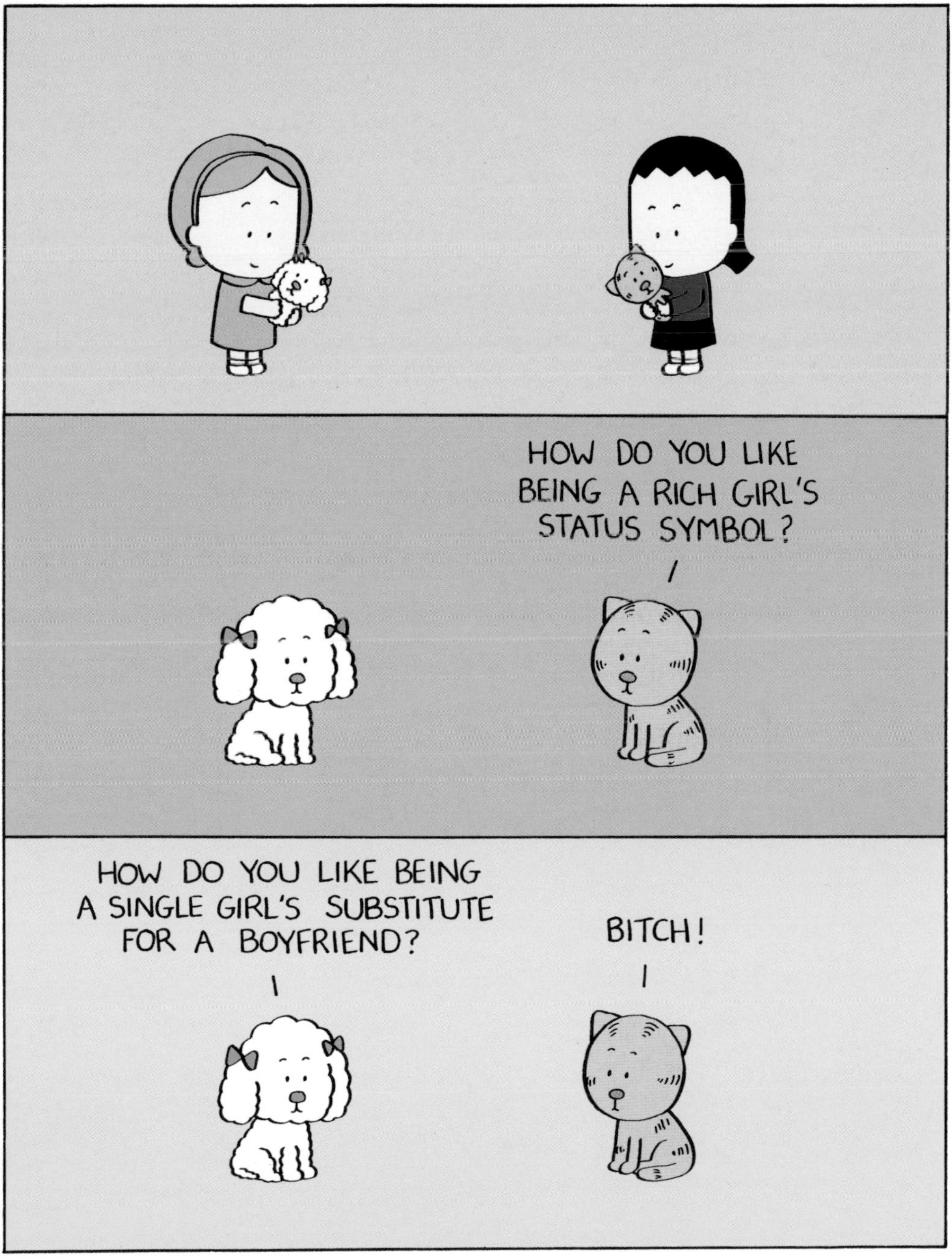
HOW DO YOU LIKE BEING A RICH GIRL'S STATUS SYMBOL?
HOW DO YOU LIKE BEING A SINGLE GIRL'S SUBSTITUTE FOR A BOYFRIEND?
BITCH!

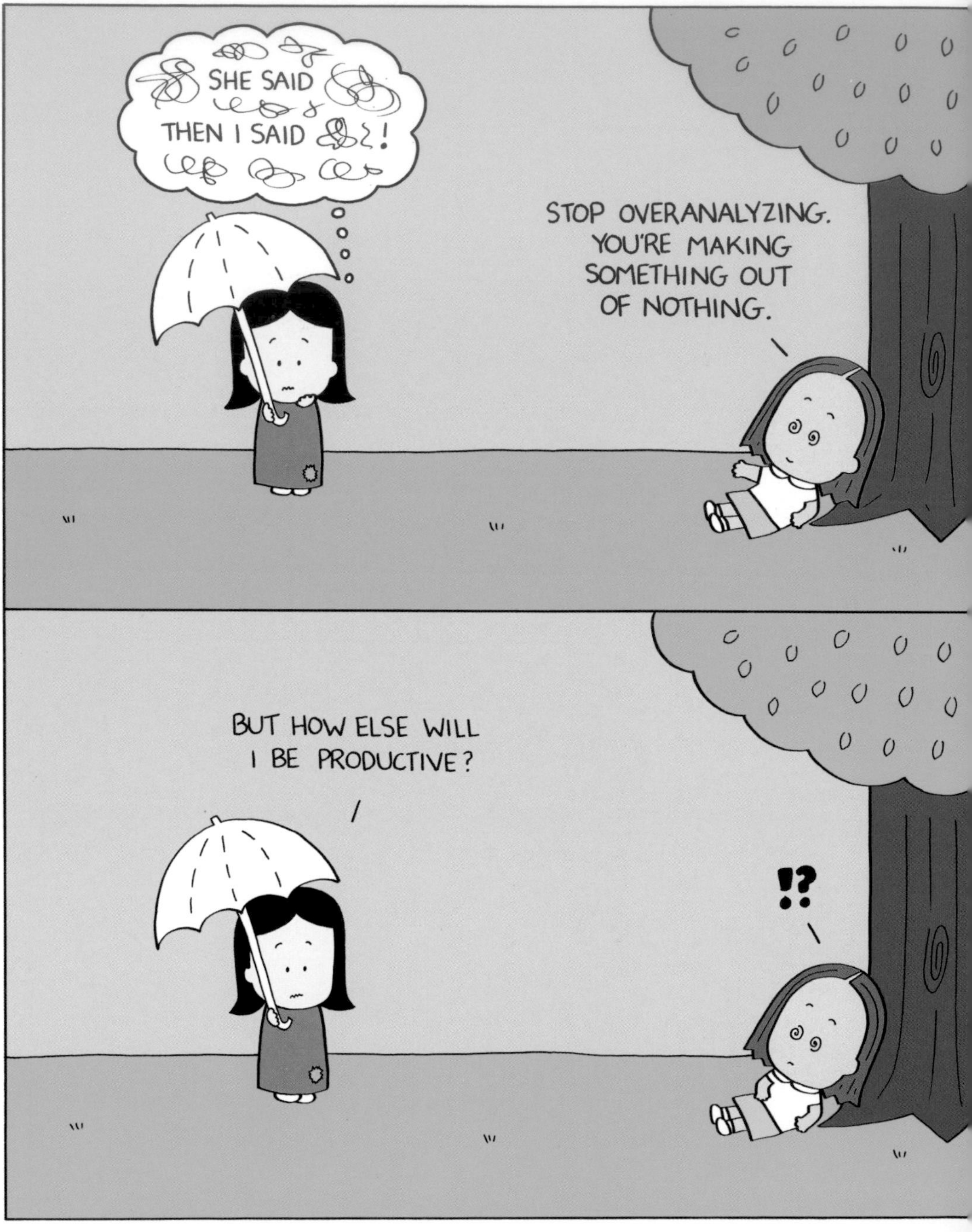
SHE SAID
THEN I SAID !
STOP OVERANALYZING. YOU'RE MAKING SOMETHING OUT OF NOTHING.
BUT HOW ELSE WILL I BE PRODUCTIVE?
!?

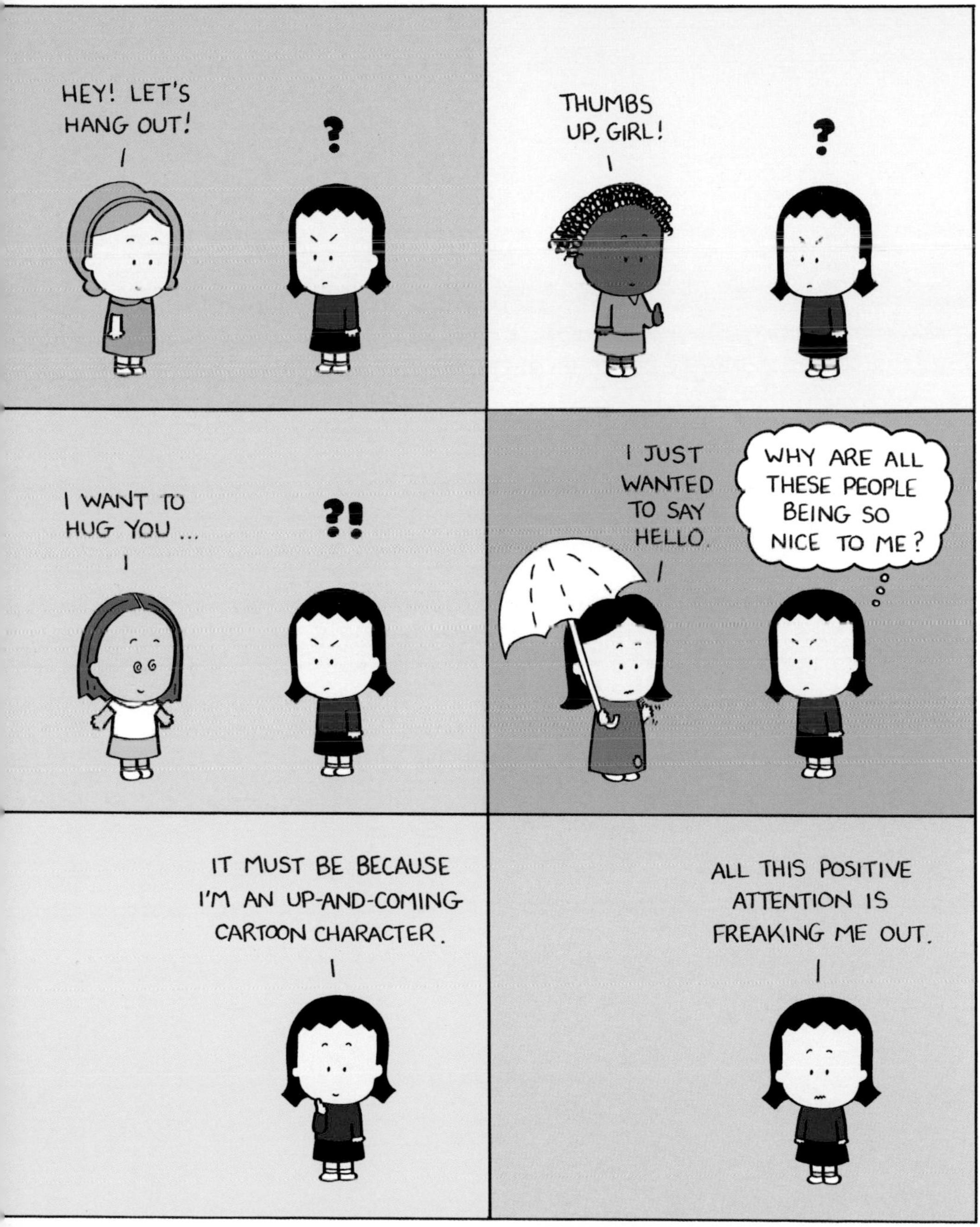

HEY! LET'S HANG OUT!
?
THUMBS UP, GIRL!
?
I WANT TO HUG YOU ...
?!
I JUST WANTED TO SAY HELLO.
WHY ARE ALL THESE PEOPLE BEING SO NICE TO ME?
IT MUST BE BECAUSE I'M AN UP-AND-COMING CARTOON CHARACTER.
ALL THIS POSITIVE ATTENTION IS FREAKING ME OUT.

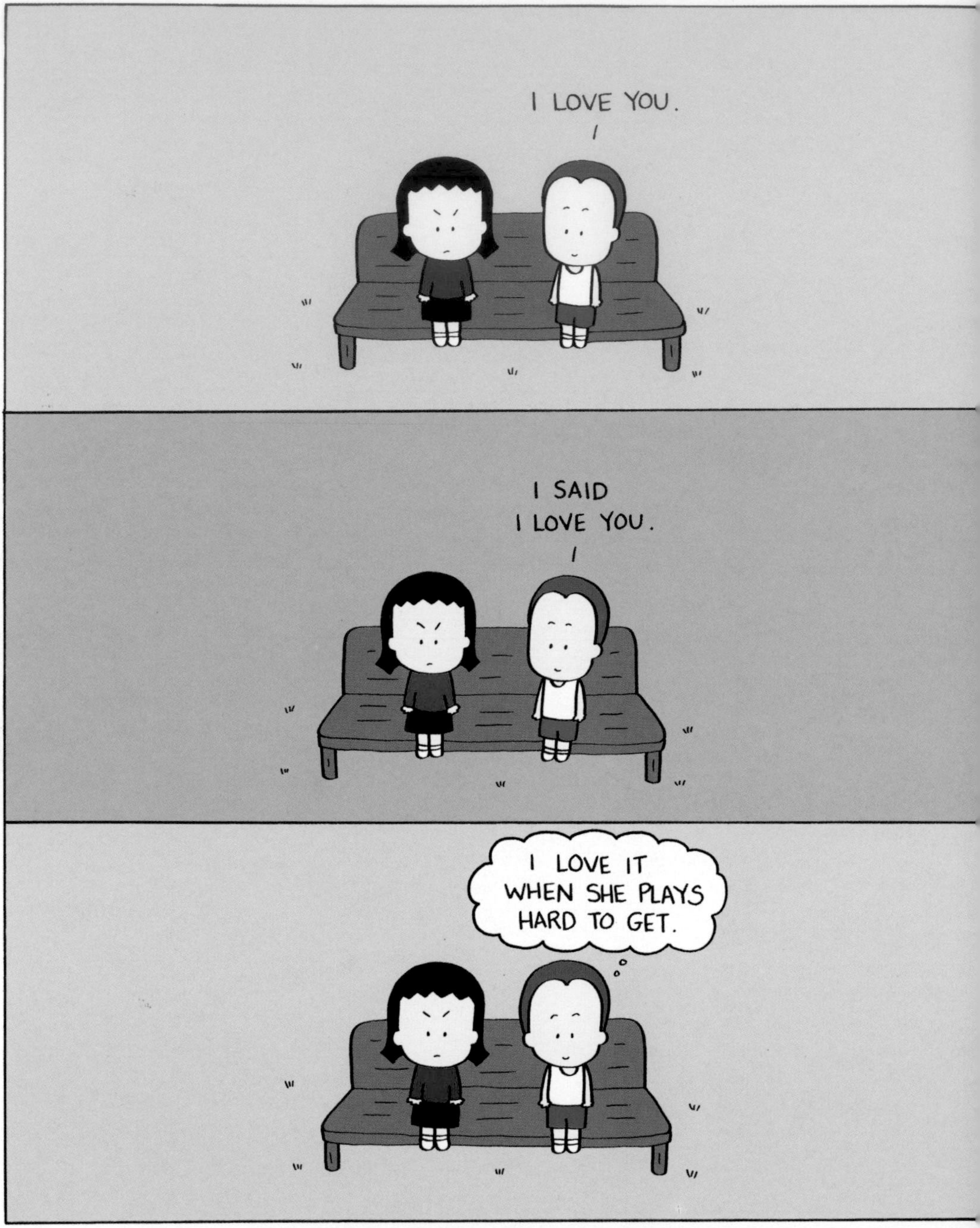
I LOVE YOU.
I SAID
I LOVE YOU.
I LOVE IT
WHEN SHE PLAYS
HARD TO GET.

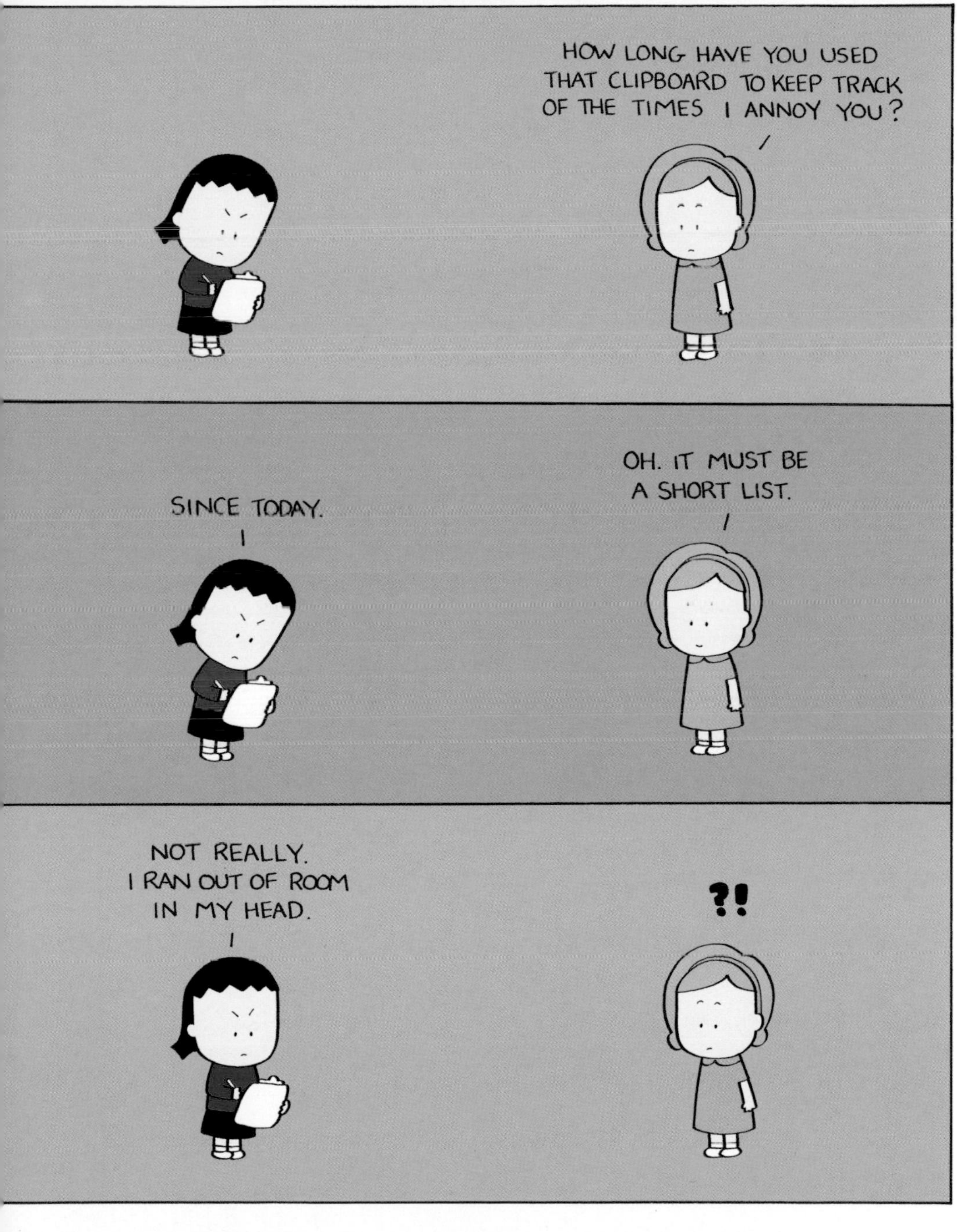
HOW LONG HAVE YOU USED THAT CLIPBOARD TO KEEP TRACK OF THE TIMES I ANNOY YOU?
SINCE TODAY.
OH. IT MUST BE A SHORT LIST.
NOT REALLY. I RAN OUT OF ROOM IN MY HEAD.
?!

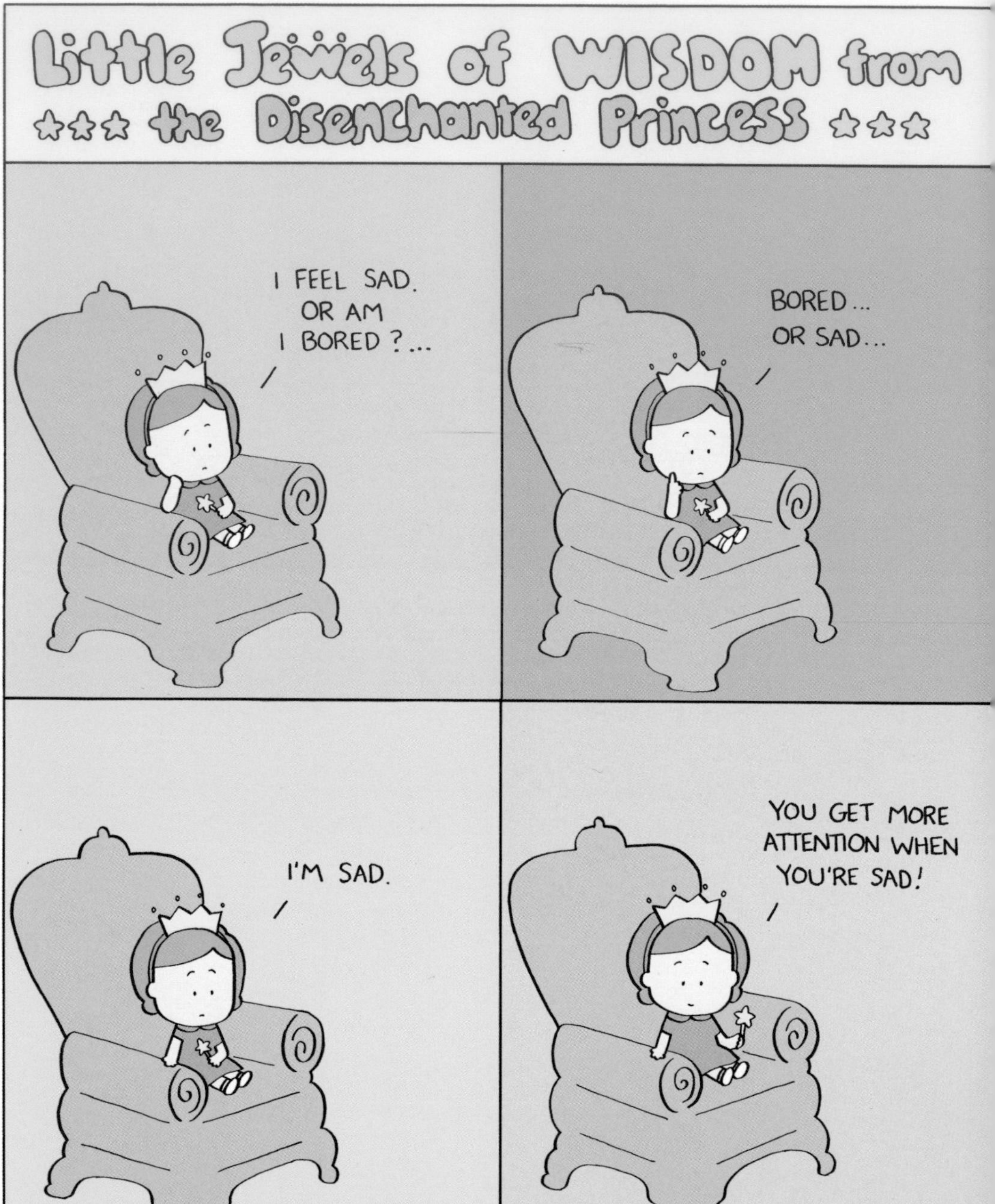
Little Jewels of WISDOM from
the Disenchanted Princess
I FEEL SAD. OR AM I BORED?...
BORED... OR SAD...
I'M SAD.
YOU GET MORE ATTENTION WHEN YOU'RE SAD!

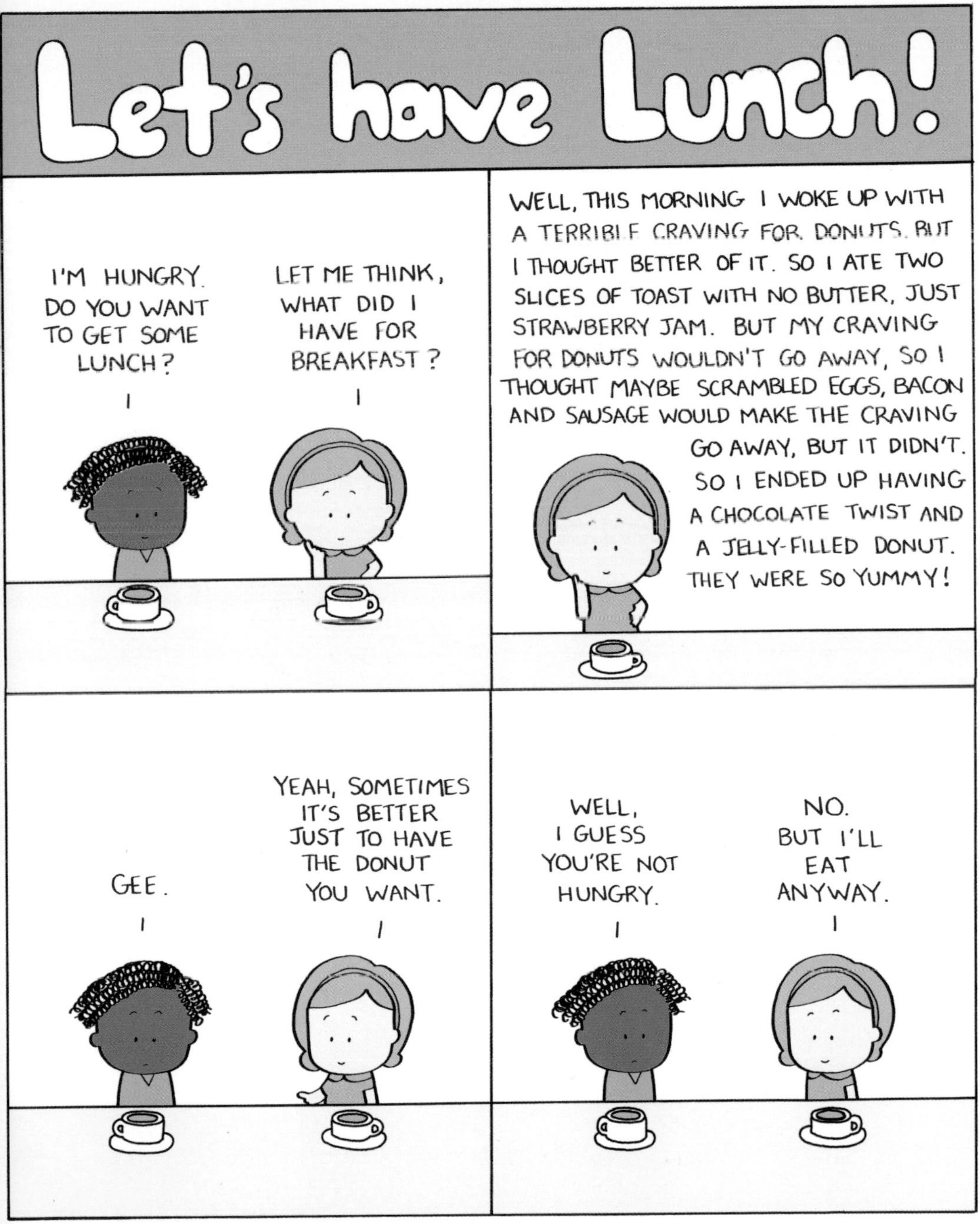
Let's have Lunch!
I'M HUNGRY. DO YOU WANT TO GET SOME LUNCH?
LET ME THINK, WHAT DID I HAVE FOR BREAKFAST?
WELL, THIS MORNING I WOKE UP WITH A TERRIBLE CRAVING FOR DONUTS. BUT I THOUGHT BETTER OF IT. SO I ATE TWO SLICES OF TOAST WITH NO BUTTER, JUST STRAWBERRY JAM. BUT MY CRAVING FOR DONUTS WOULDN'T GO AWAY, SO I THOUGHT MAYBE SCRAMBLED EGGS, BACON AND SAUSAGE WOULD MAKE THE CRAVING GO AWAY, BUT IT DIDN'T. SO I ENDED UP HAVING A CHOCOLATE TWIST AND A JELLY-FILLED DONUT. THEY WERE SO YUMMY!
GEE.
YEAH, SOMETIMES IT'S BETTER JUST TO HAVE THE DONUT YOU WANT.
WELL, I GUESS YOU'RE NOT HUNGRY.
NO. BUT I'LL EAT ANYWAY.

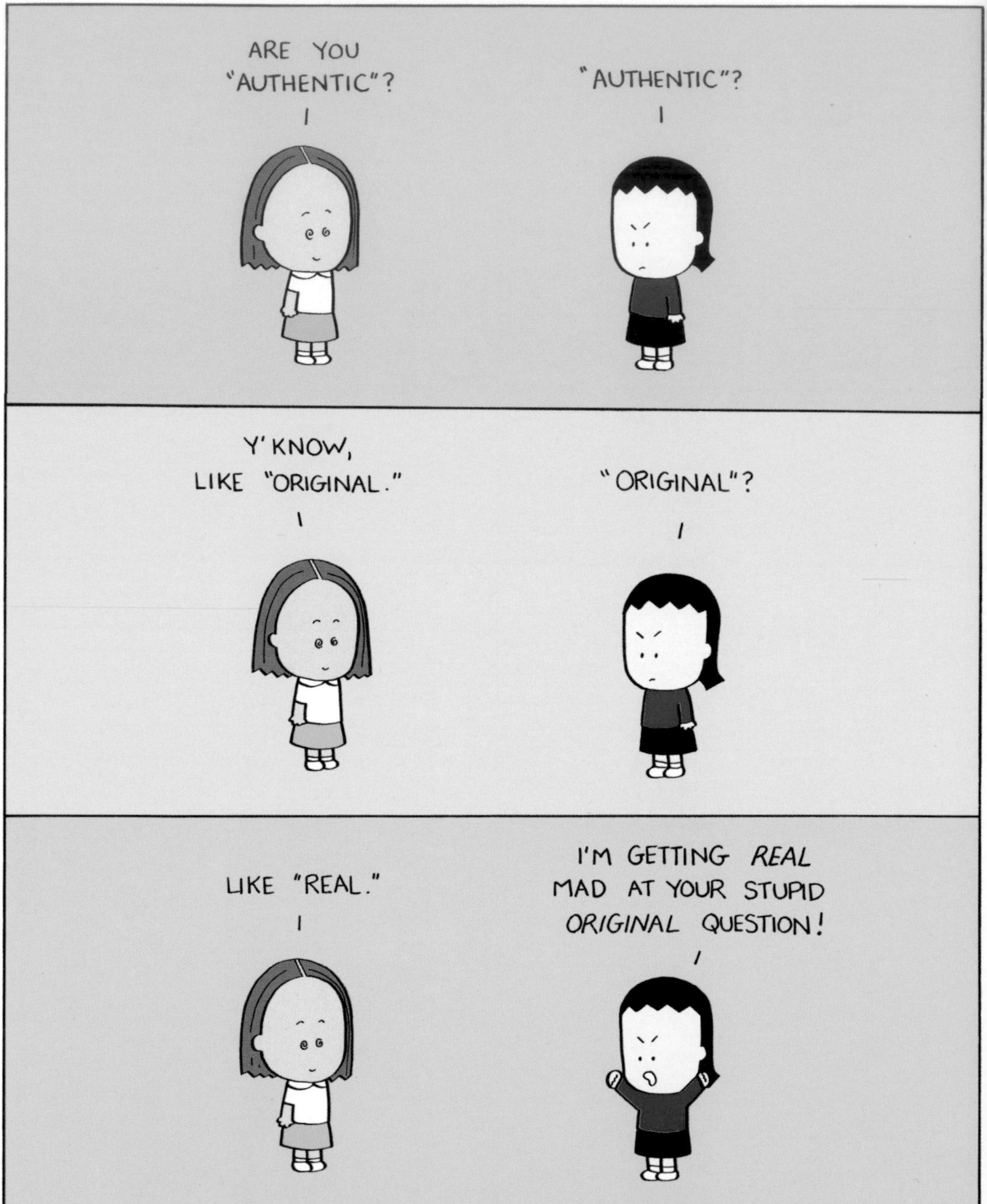
ARE YOU "AUTHENTIC"?
"AUTHENTIC"?
Y'KNOW, LIKE "ORIGINAL."
"ORIGINAL"?
LIKE "REAL."
I'M GETTING *REAL* MAD AT YOUR STUPID *ORIGINAL* QUESTION!

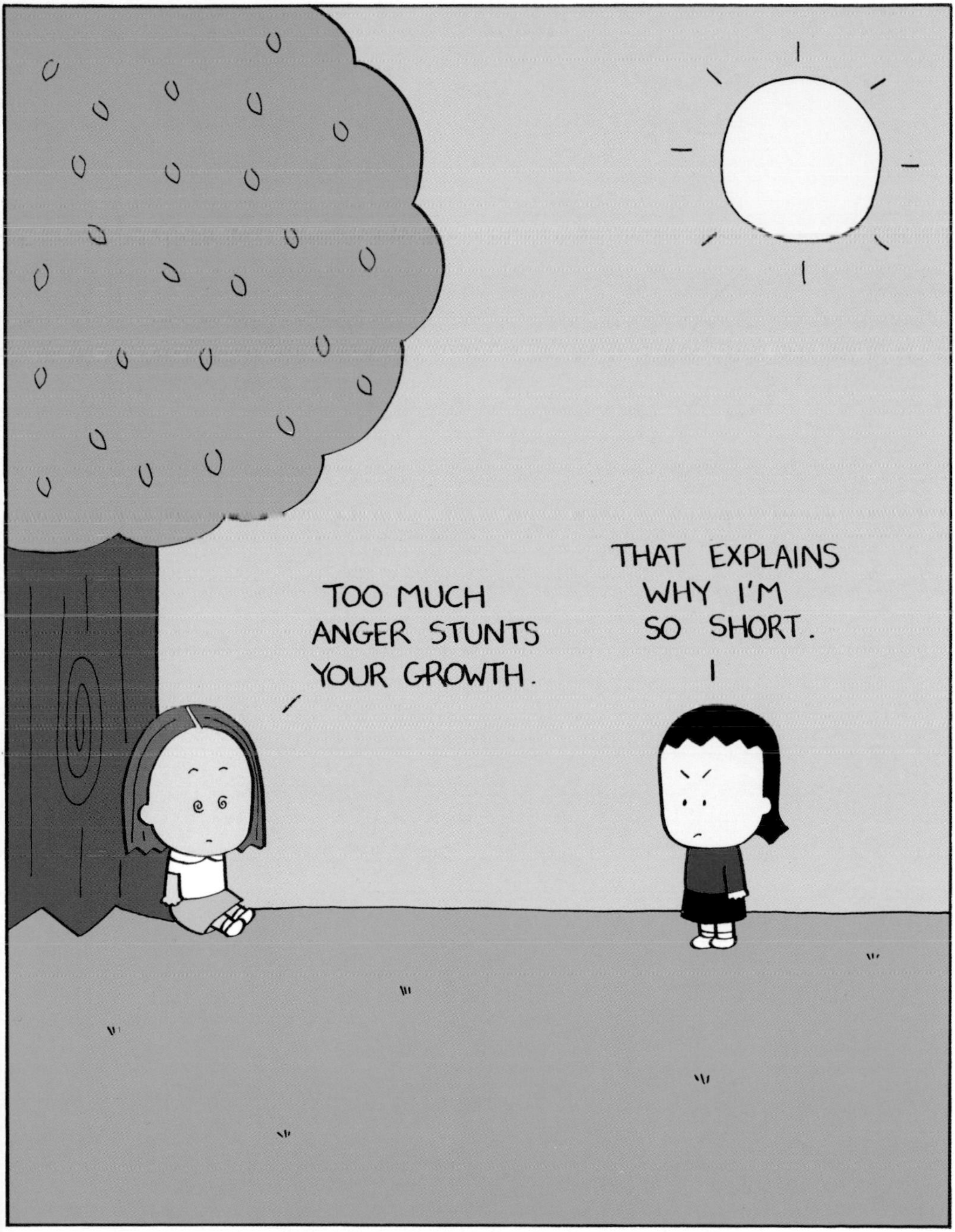
TOO MUCH ANGER STUNTS YOUR GROWTH.
THAT EXPLAINS WHY I'M SO SHORT.

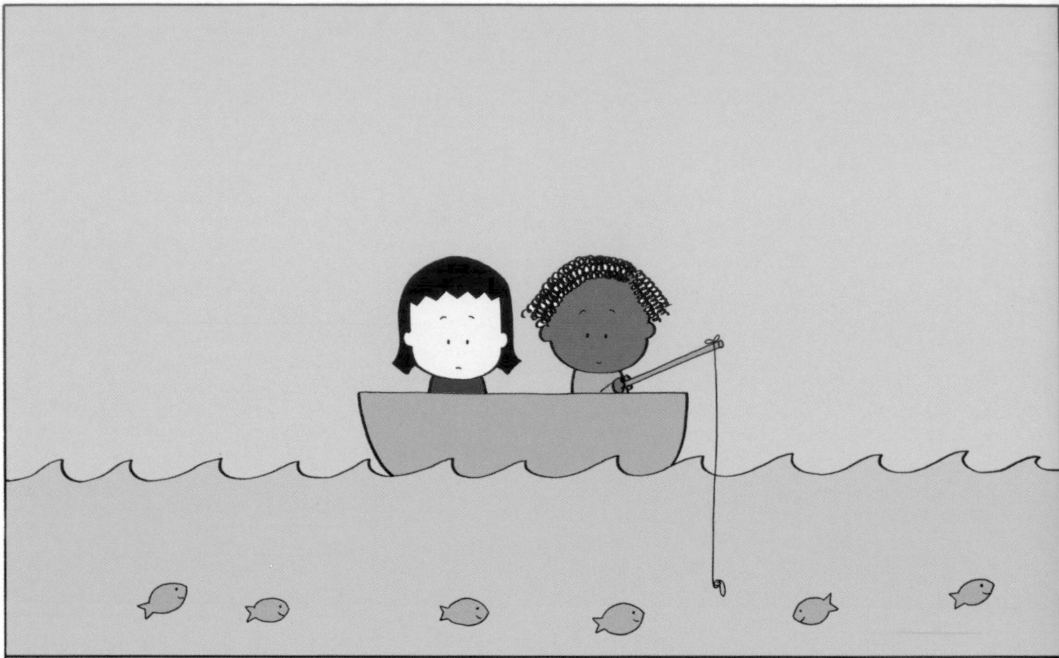
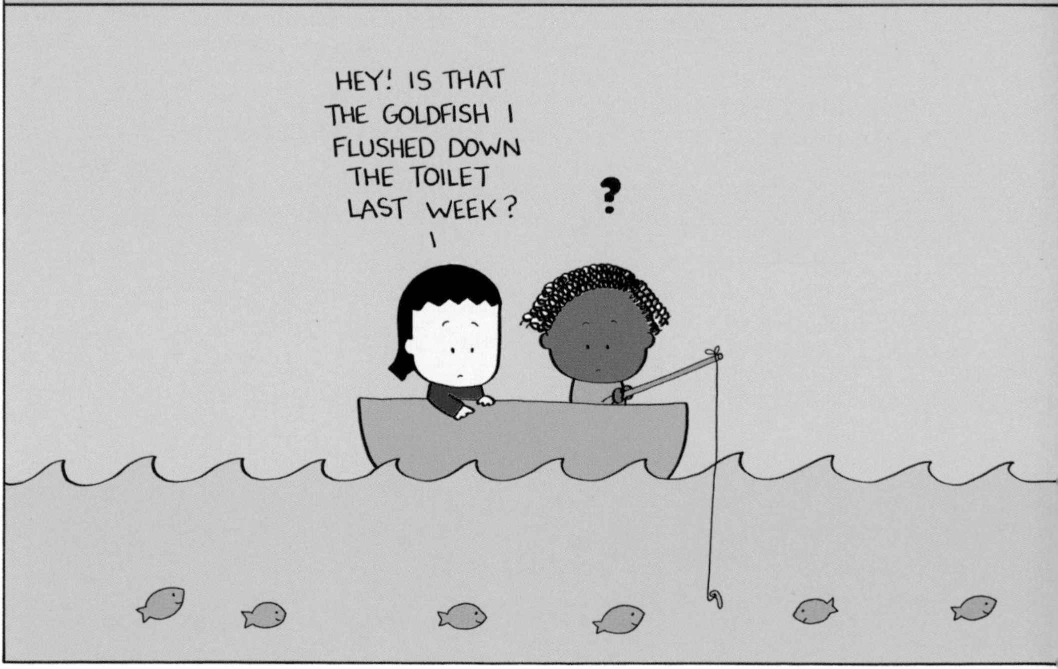
HEY! IS THAT THE GOLDFISH I FLUSHED DOWN THE TOILET LAST WEEK?
?

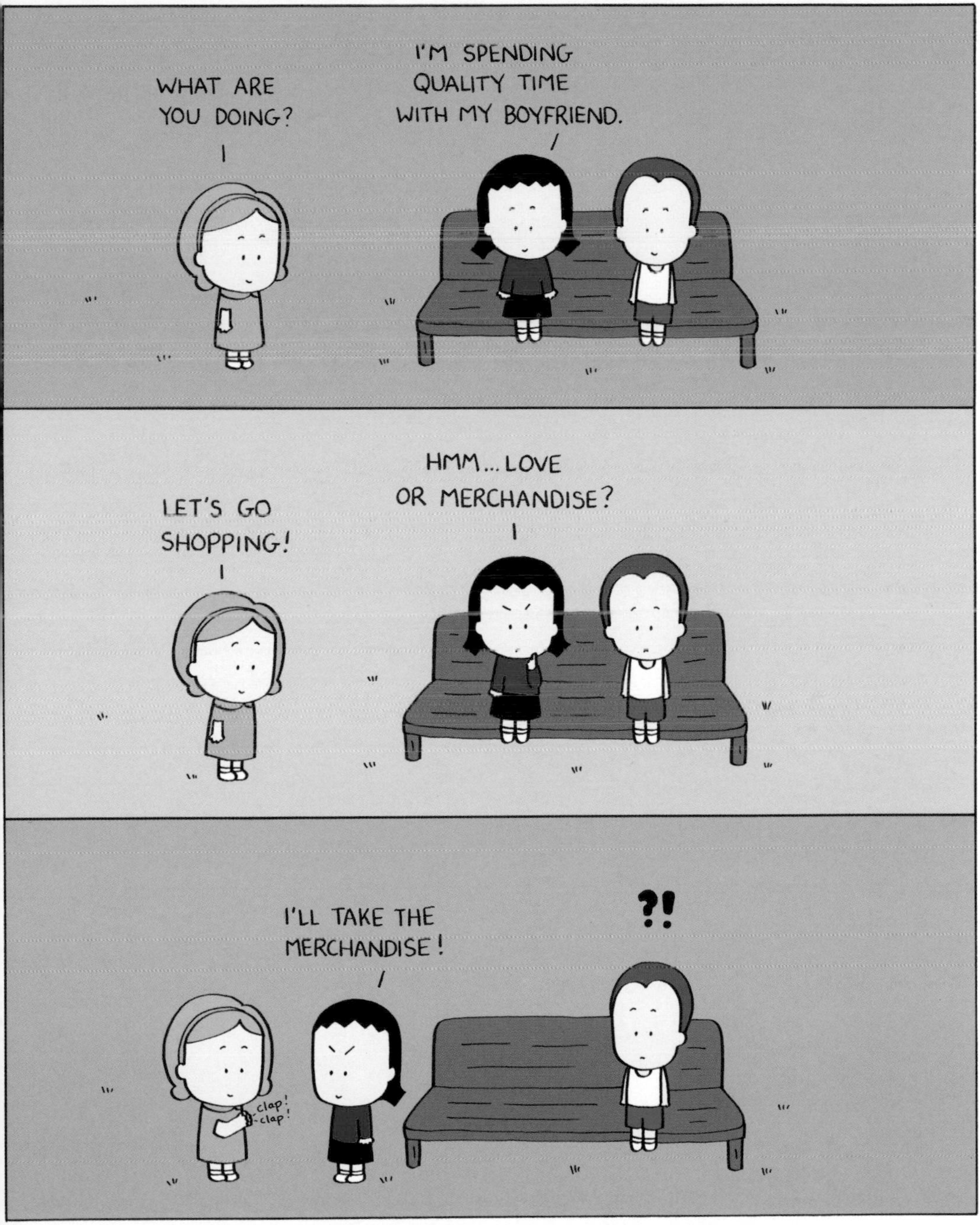
WHAT ARE YOU DOING?
I'M SPENDING QUALITY TIME WITH MY BOYFRIEND.
LET'S GO SHOPPING!
HMM... LOVE OR MERCHANDISE?
I'LL TAKE THE MERCHANDISE!
clap! clap!
?!

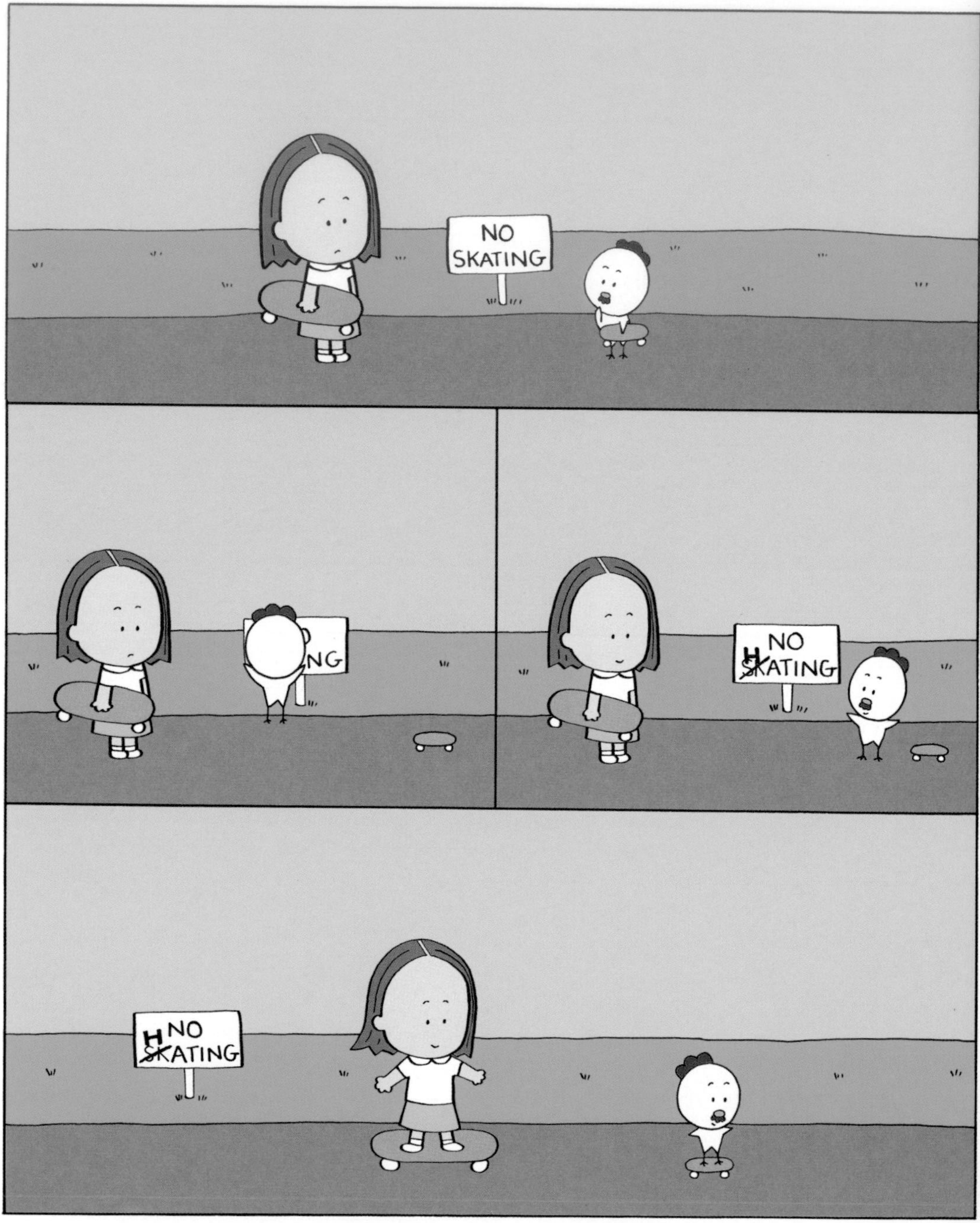
NO
SKATING
NG
H
NO
SKATING
H
NO
SKATING

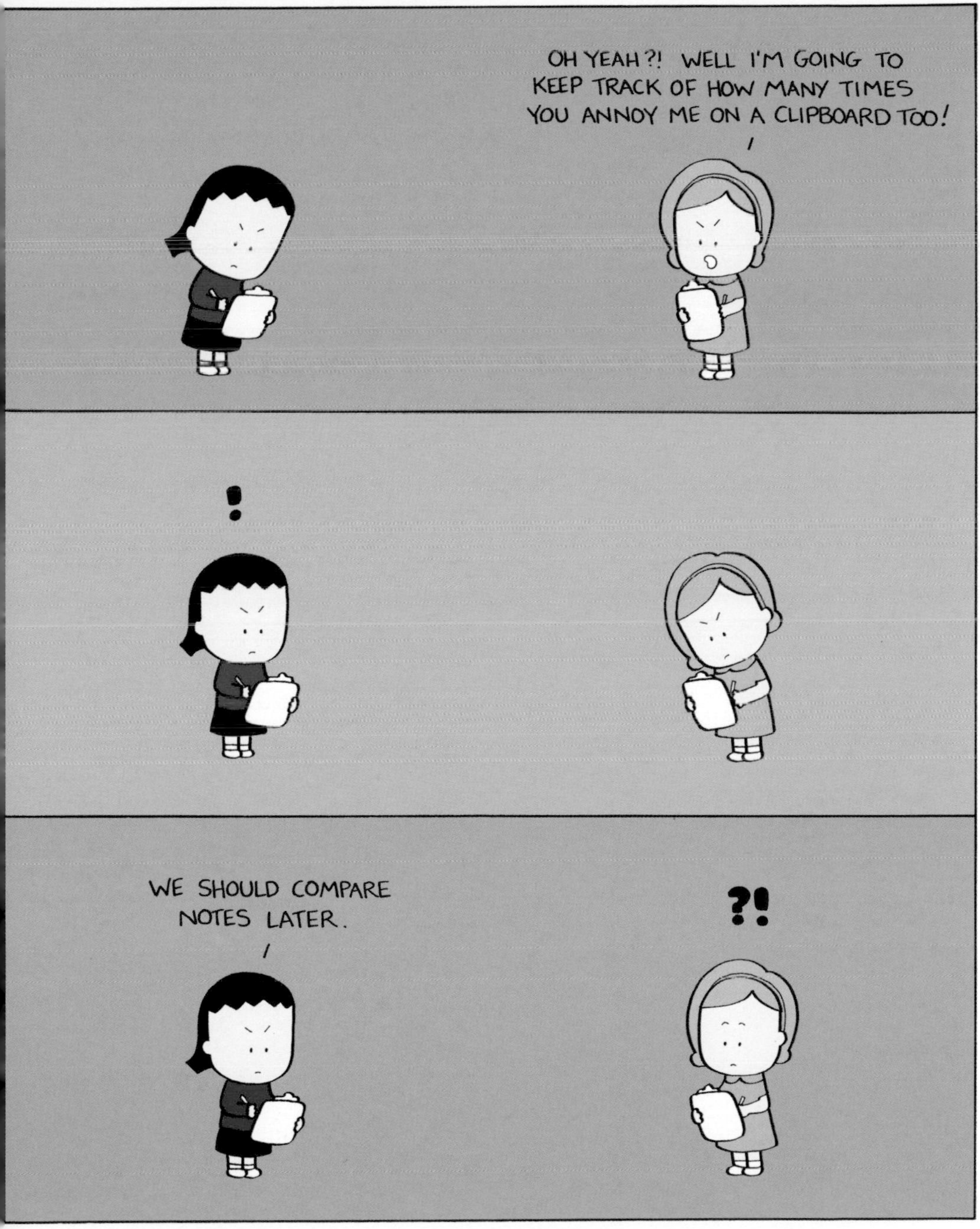
OH YEAH?! WELL I'M GOING TO KEEP TRACK OF HOW MANY TIMES YOU ANNOY ME ON A CLIPBOARD TOO!
!
WE SHOULD COMPARE NOTES LATER.
?!

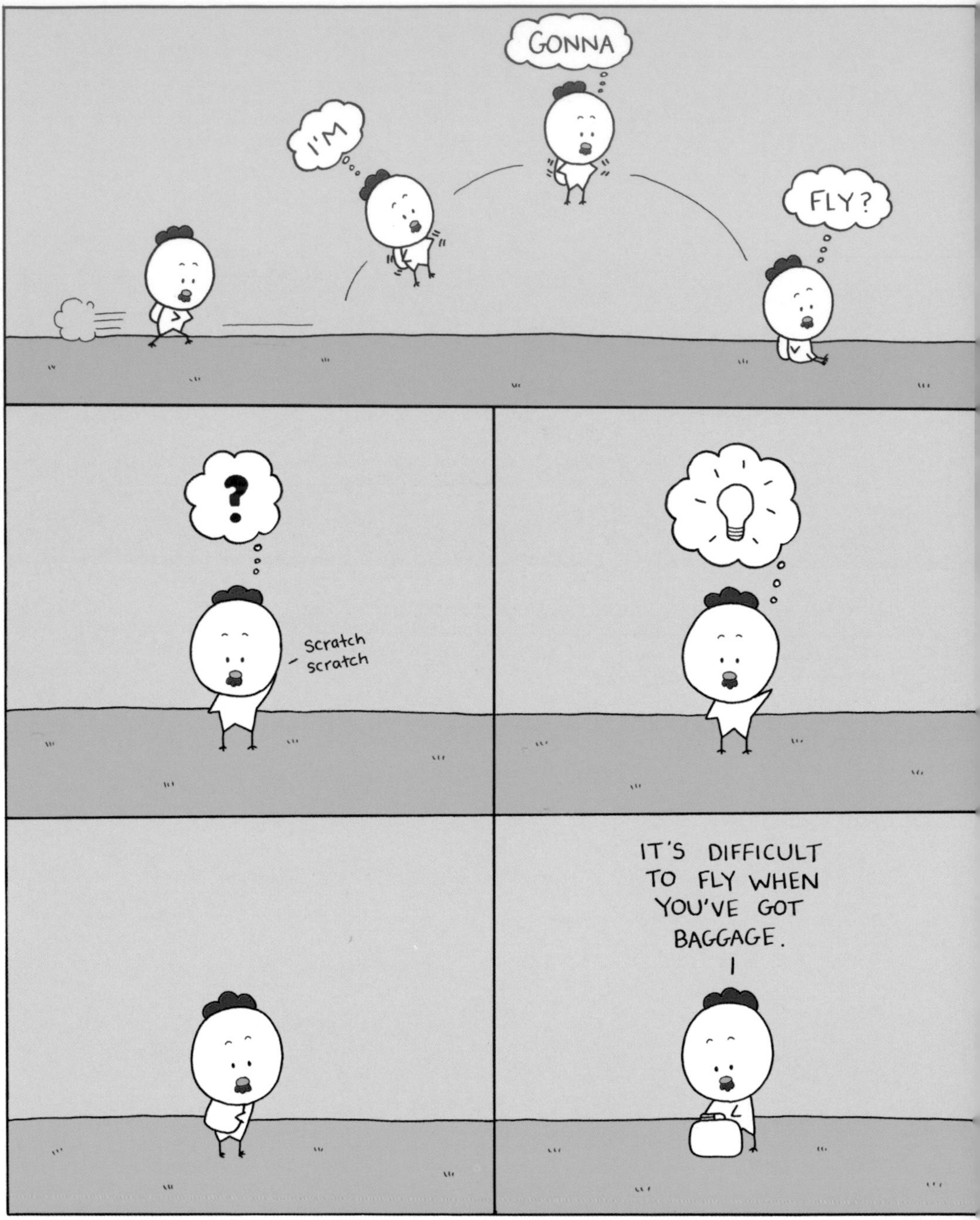
I'M
GONNA
FLY?
?
scratch
scratch
IT'S DIFFICULT TO FLY WHEN YOU'VE GOT BAGGAGE.

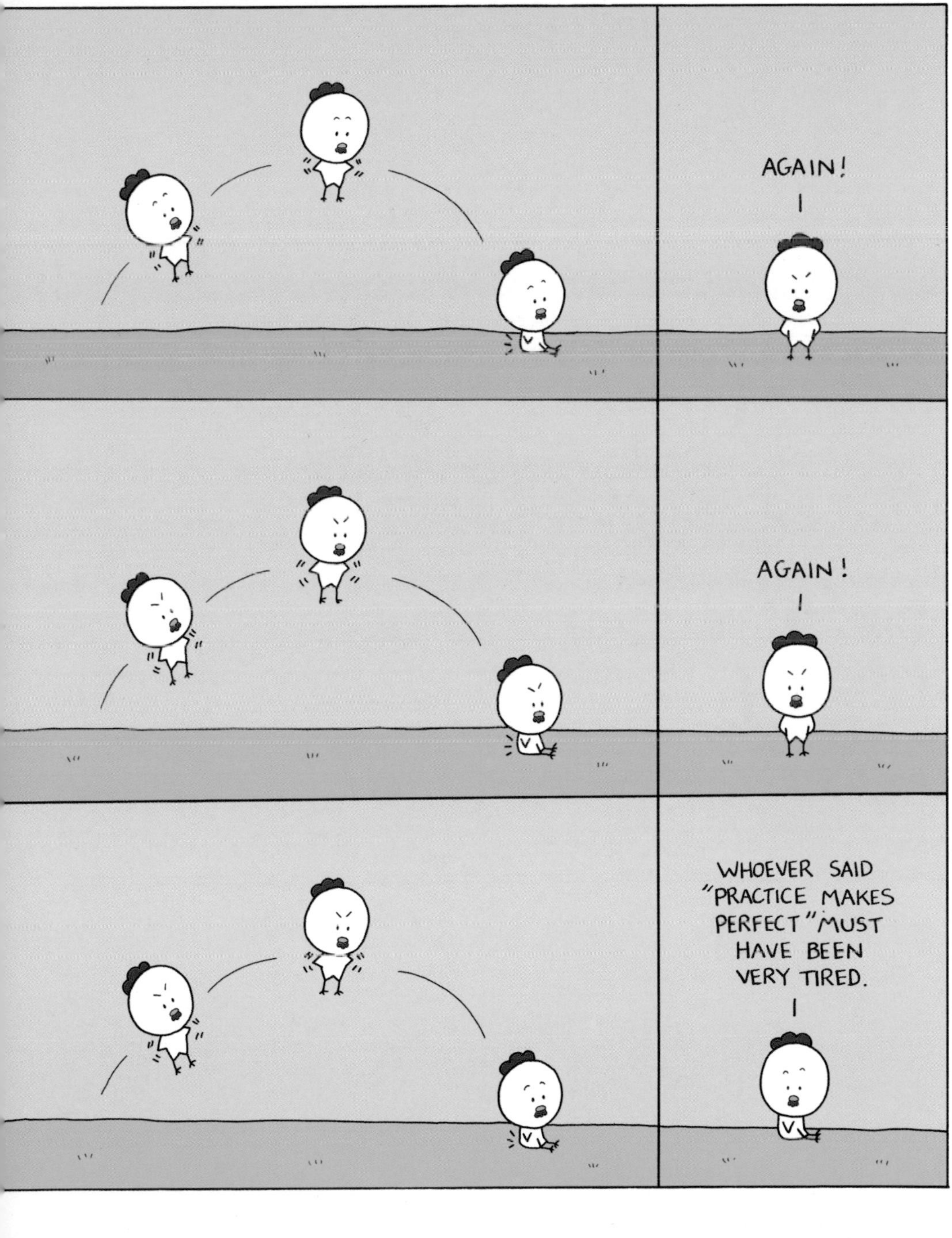
AGAIN!
AGAIN!
WHOEVER SAID "PRACTICE MAKES PERFECT" MUST HAVE BEEN VERY TIRED.

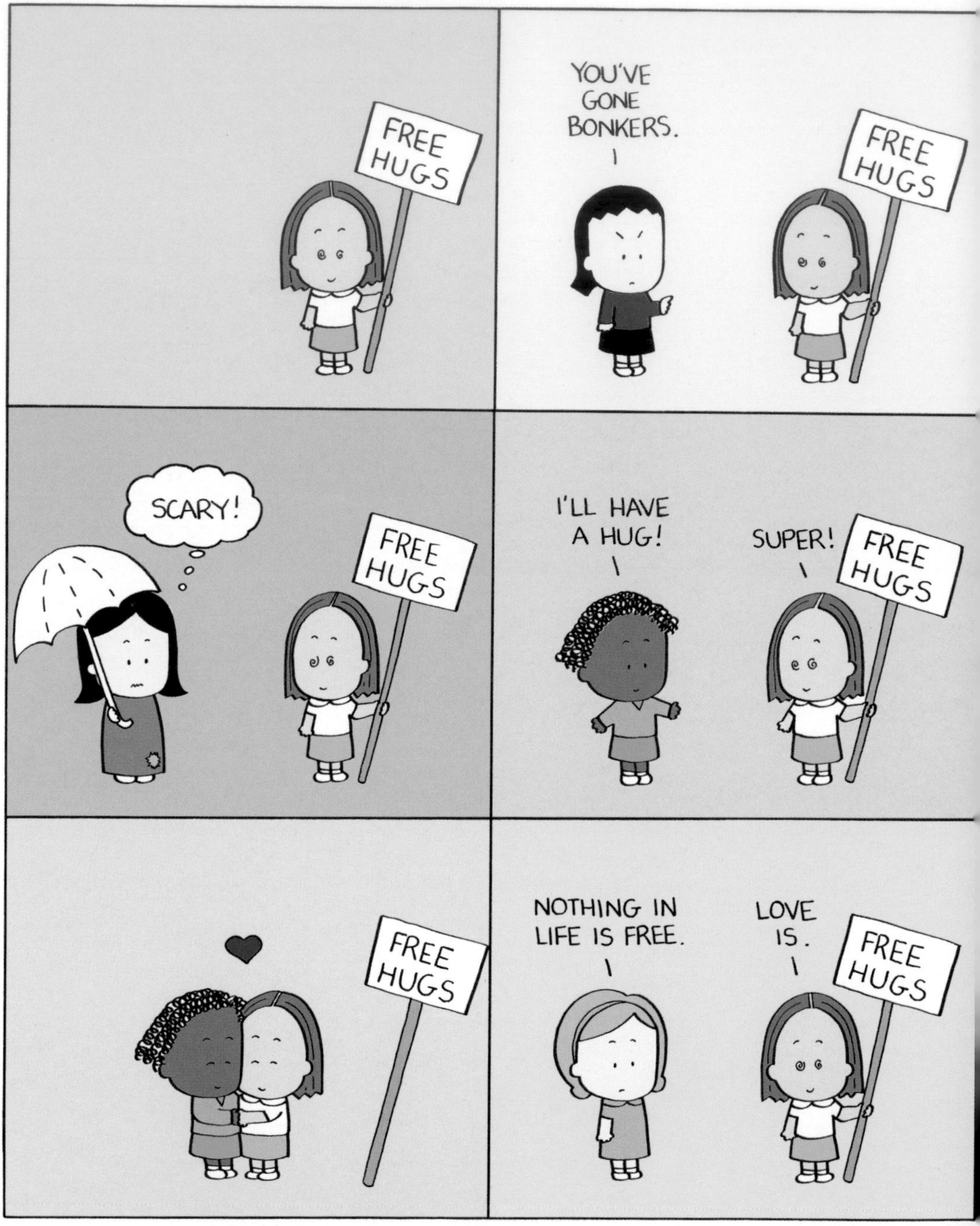
FREE HUGS
YOU'VE GONE BONKERS.
FREE HUGS
SCARY!
FREE HUGS
I'LL HAVE A HUG!
SUPER!
FREE HUGS
FREE HUGS
NOTHING IN LIFE IS FREE.
LOVE IS.
FREE HUGS

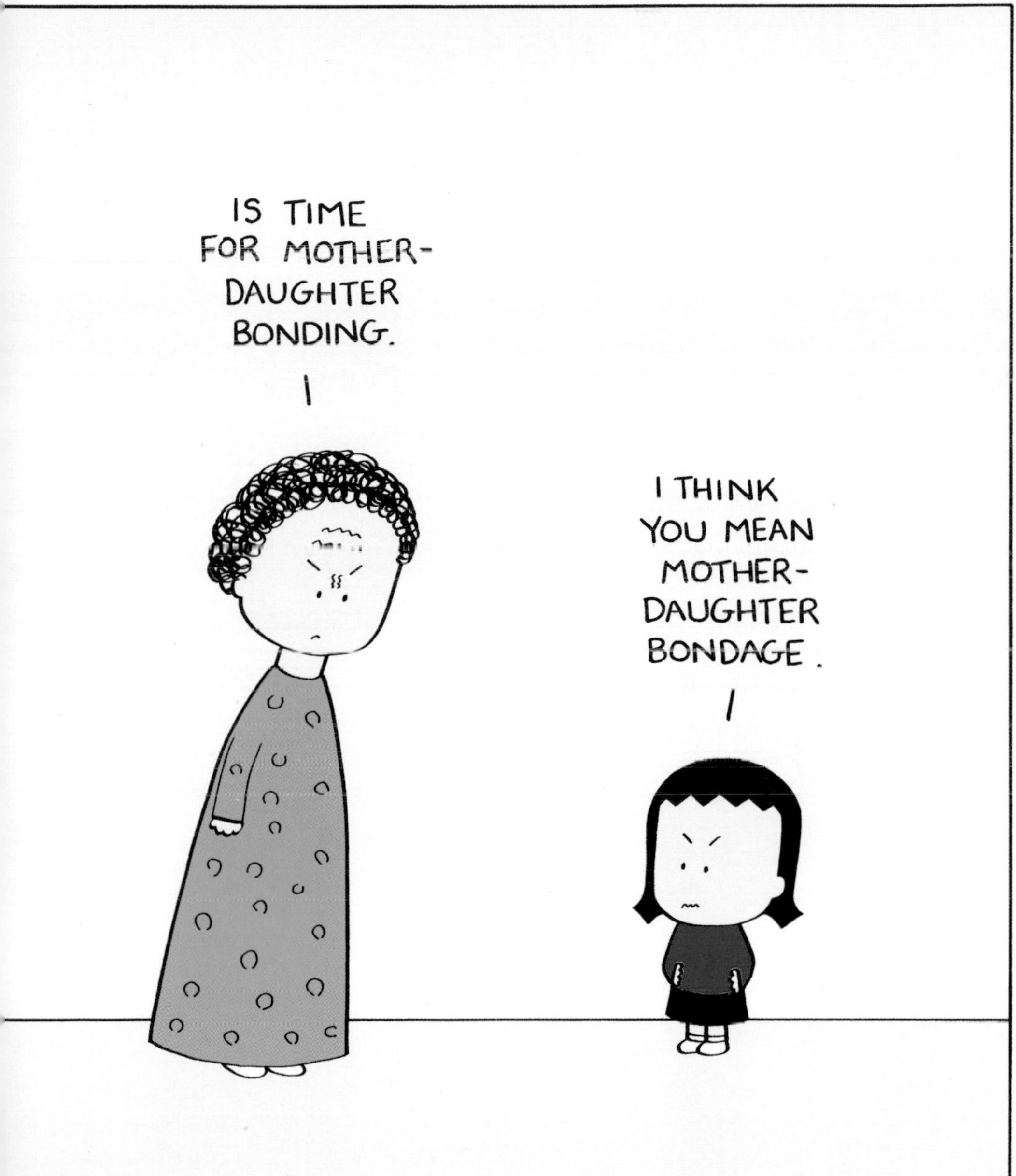
IS TIME FOR MOTHER-DAUGHTER BONDING.
I THINK YOU MEAN MOTHER-DAUGHTER BONDAGE.

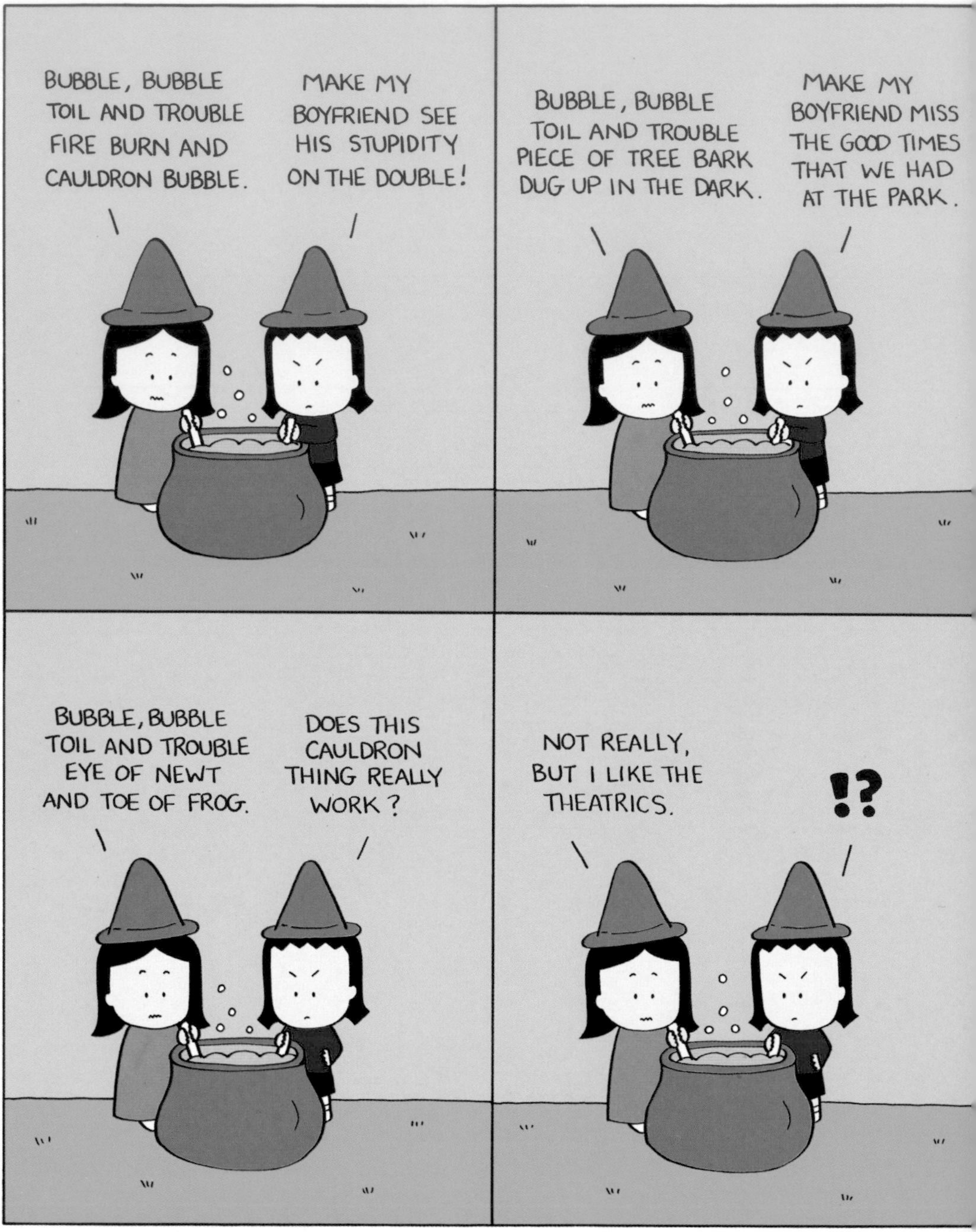
BUBBLE, BUBBLE TOIL AND TROUBLE FIRE BURN AND CAULDRON BUBBLE.
MAKE MY BOYFRIEND SEE HIS STUPIDITY ON THE DOUBLE!
BUBBLE, BUBBLE TOIL AND TROUBLE PIECE OF TREE BARK DUG UP IN THE DARK.
MAKE MY BOYFRIEND MISS THE GOOD TIMES THAT WE HAD AT THE PARK.
BUBBLE, BUBBLE TOIL AND TROUBLE EYE OF NEWT AND TOE OF FROG.
DOES THIS CAULDRON THING REALLY WORK?
NOT REALLY, BUT I LIKE THE THEATRICS.
!?

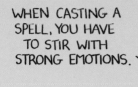
WHEN CASTING A SPELL, YOU HAVE TO STIR WITH STRONG EMOTIONS.

OKAY.

BUBBLE, BUBBLE TOIL AND TROUBLE...

MAKE MY BOYFRIEND CHOKE ON HIS LIES ON THE DOUBLE!

WE'RE SUPPOSED TO BE GOOD WITCHES.

WHAT FUN IS THAT?

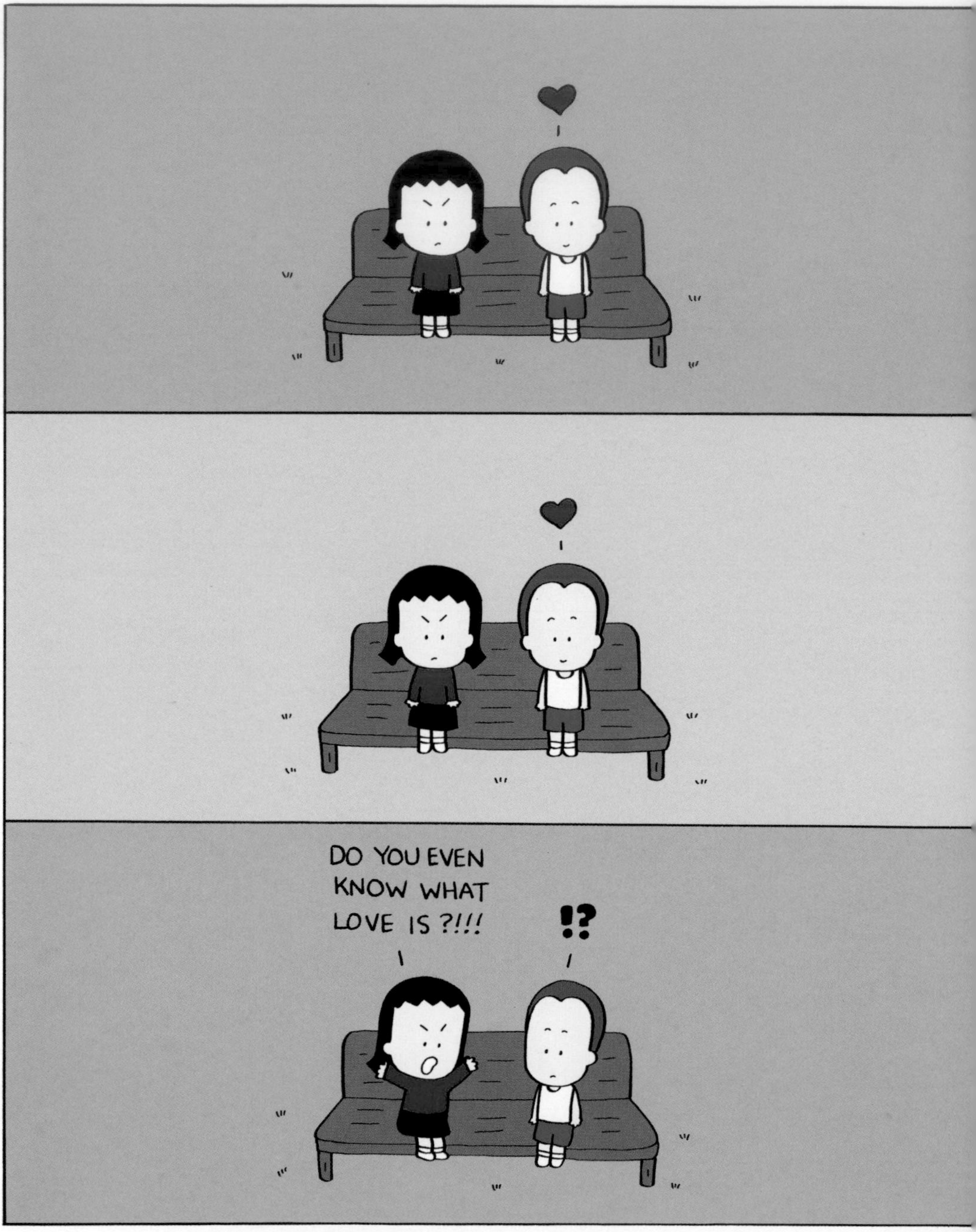
DO YOU EVEN KNOW WHAT LOVE IS ?!!!
!?

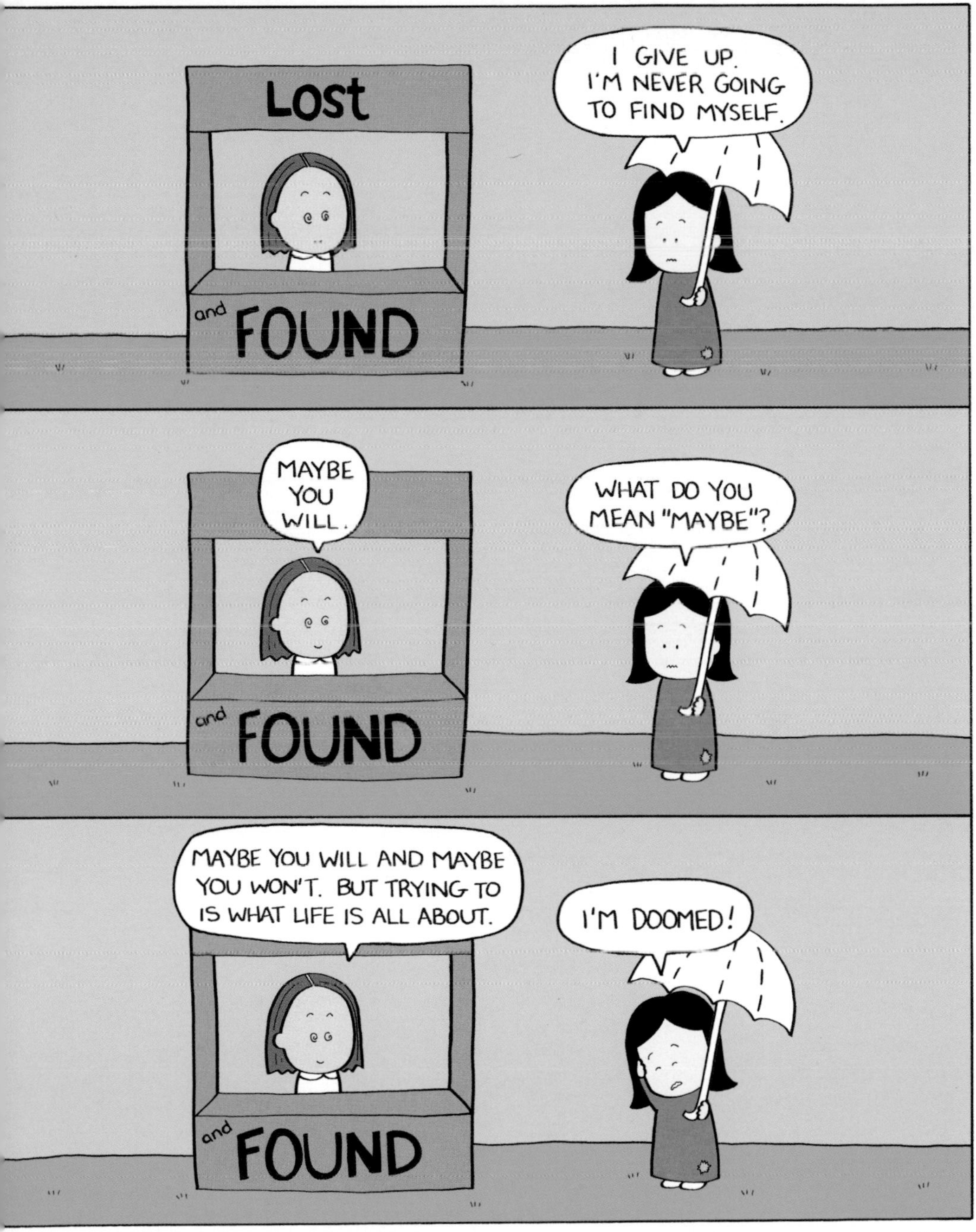
Lost
and FOUND
I GIVE UP. I'M NEVER GOING TO FIND MYSELF.
and FOUND
MAYBE YOU WILL.
WHAT DO YOU MEAN "MAYBE"?
and FOUND
MAYBE YOU WILL AND MAYBE YOU WON'T. BUT TRYING TO IS WHAT LIFE IS ALL ABOUT.
I'M DOOMED!

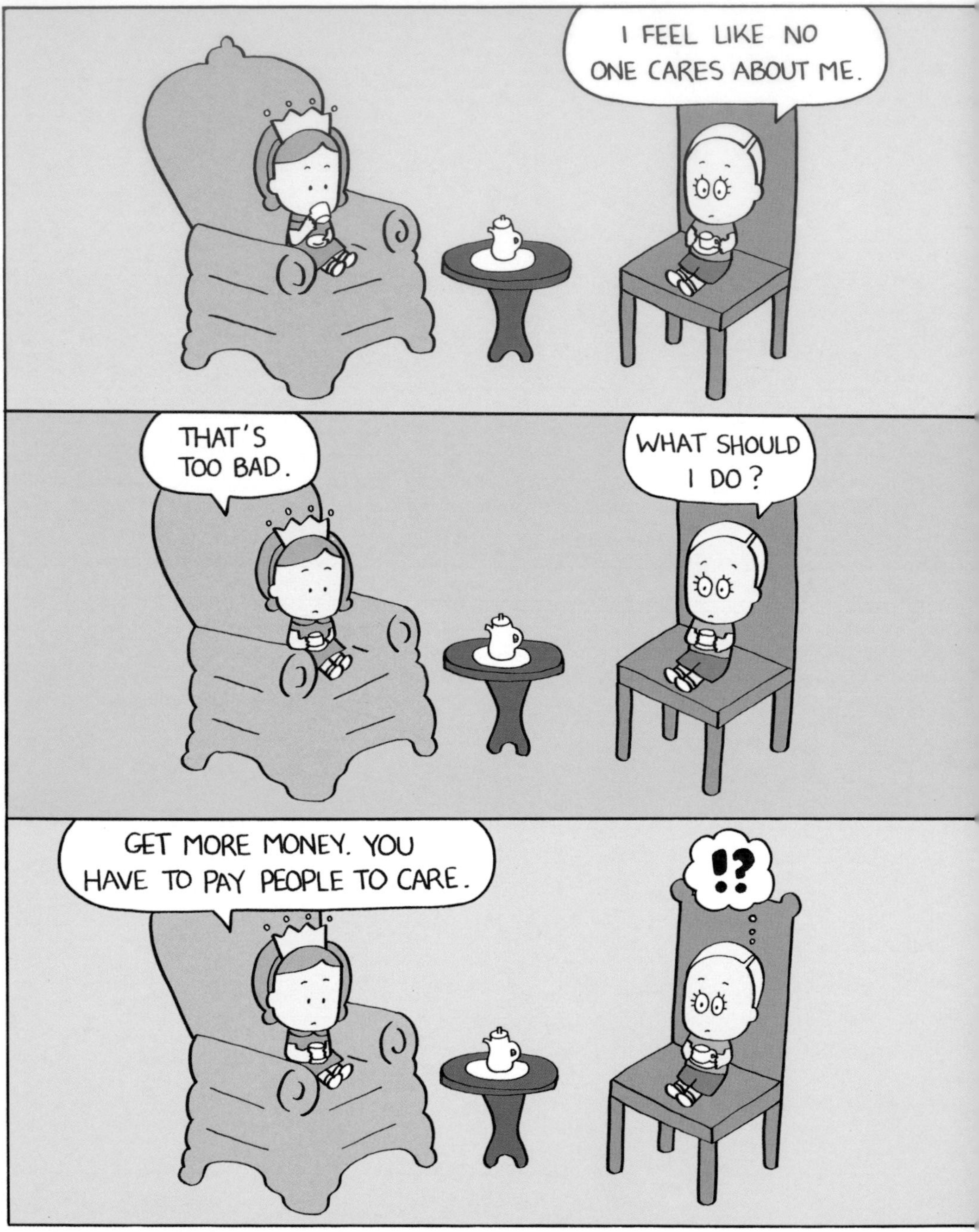
I FEEL LIKE NO ONE CARES ABOUT ME.
THAT'S TOO BAD.
WHAT SHOULD I DO?
GET MORE MONEY. YOU HAVE TO PAY PEOPLE TO CARE.
!?

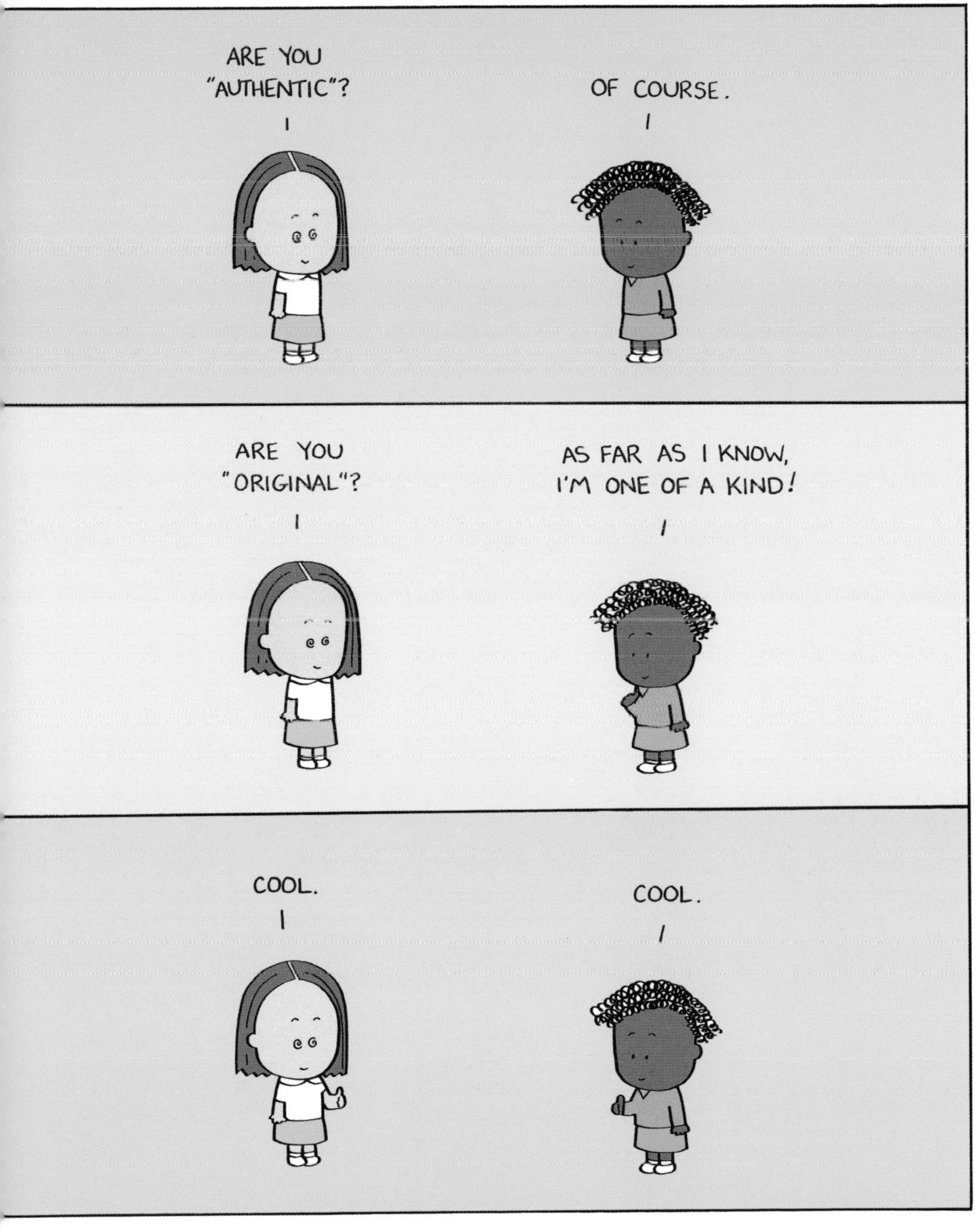
ARE YOU "AUTHENTIC"?
OF COURSE.
ARE YOU "ORIGINAL"?
AS FAR AS I KNOW, I'M ONE OF A KIND!
COOL.
COOL.

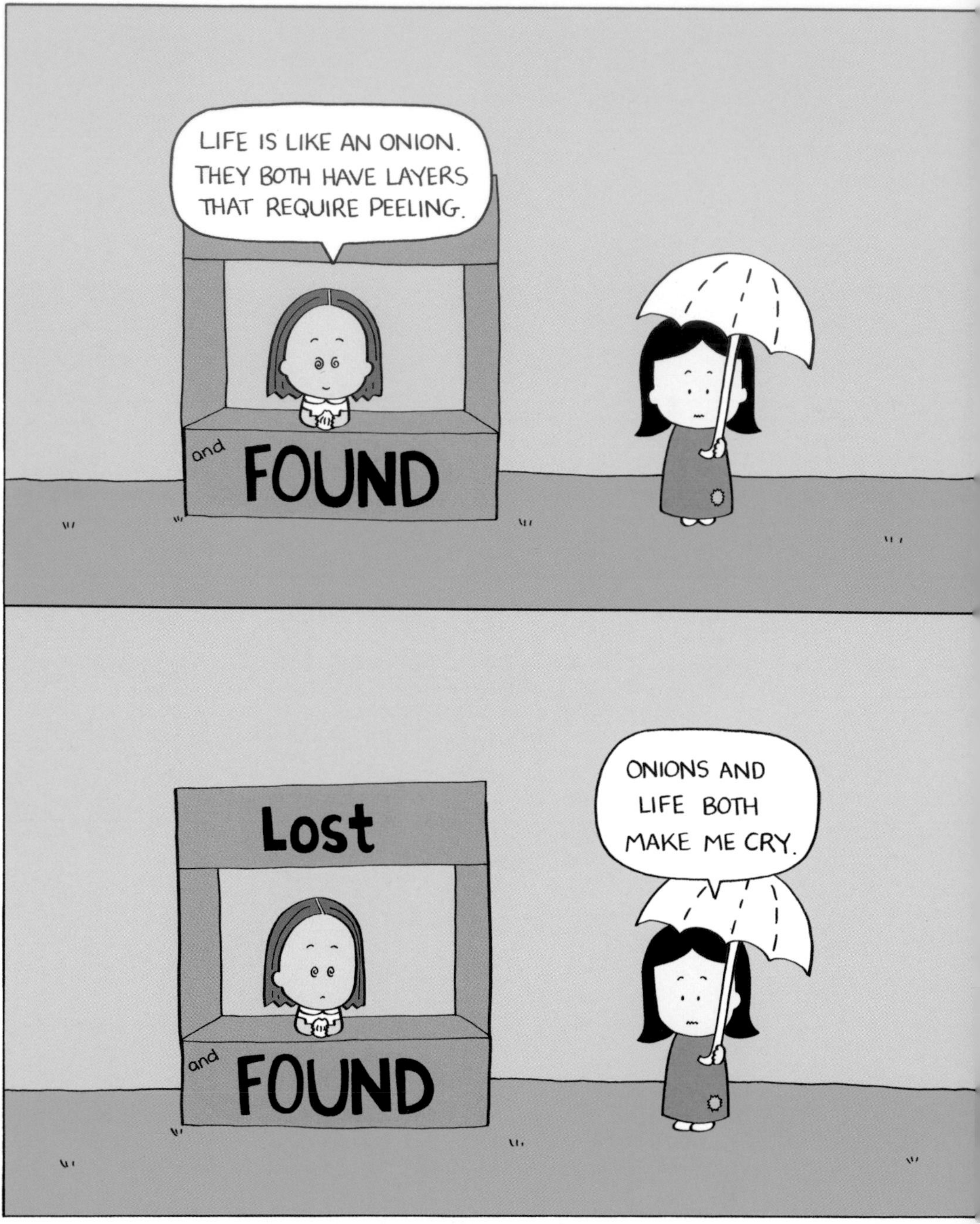
LIFE IS LIKE AN ONION. THEY BOTH HAVE LAYERS THAT REQUIRE PEELING.
and
FOUND
Lost
and
FOUND
ONIONS AND LIFE BOTH MAKE ME CRY.

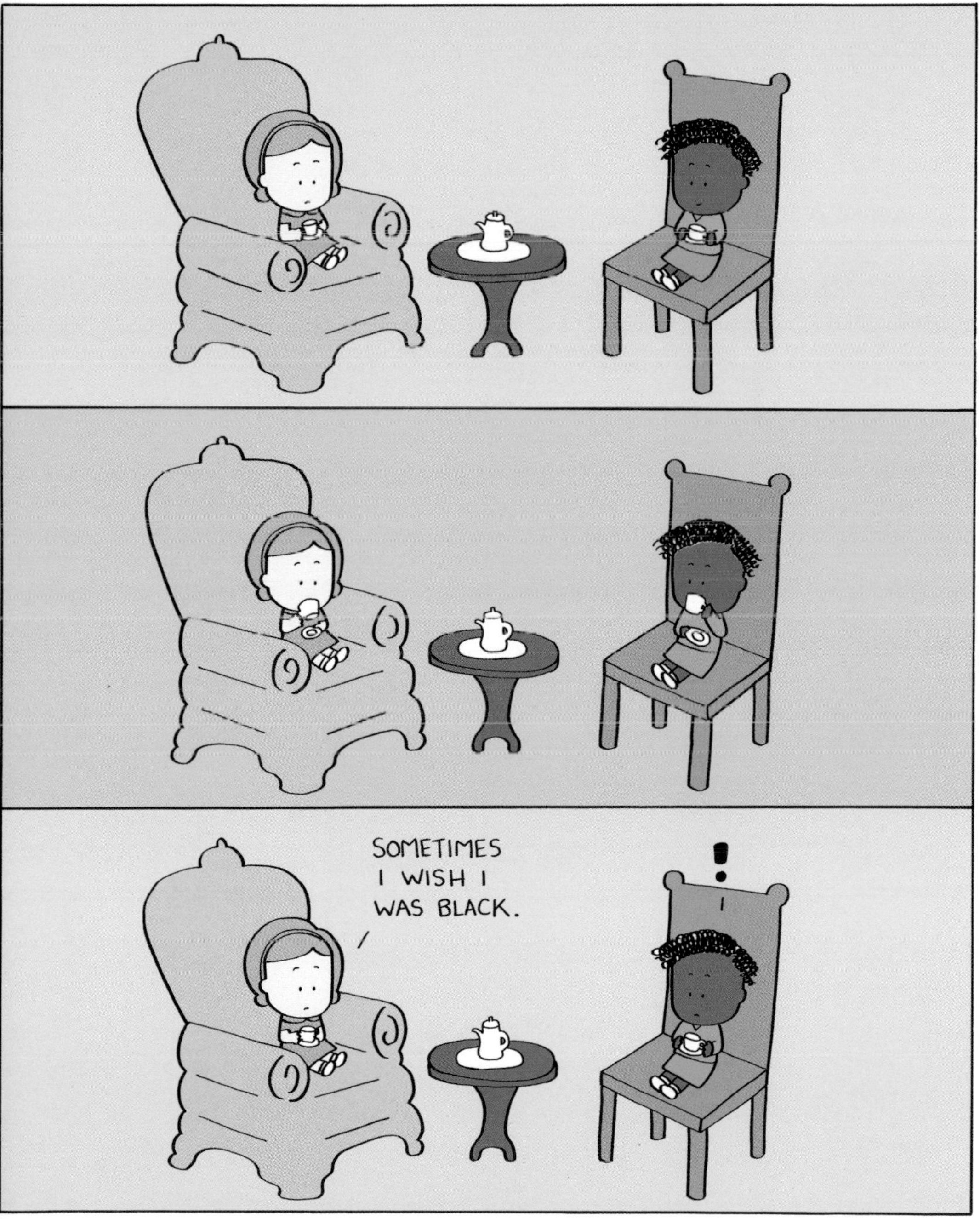
SOMETIMES I WISH I WAS BLACK.
!

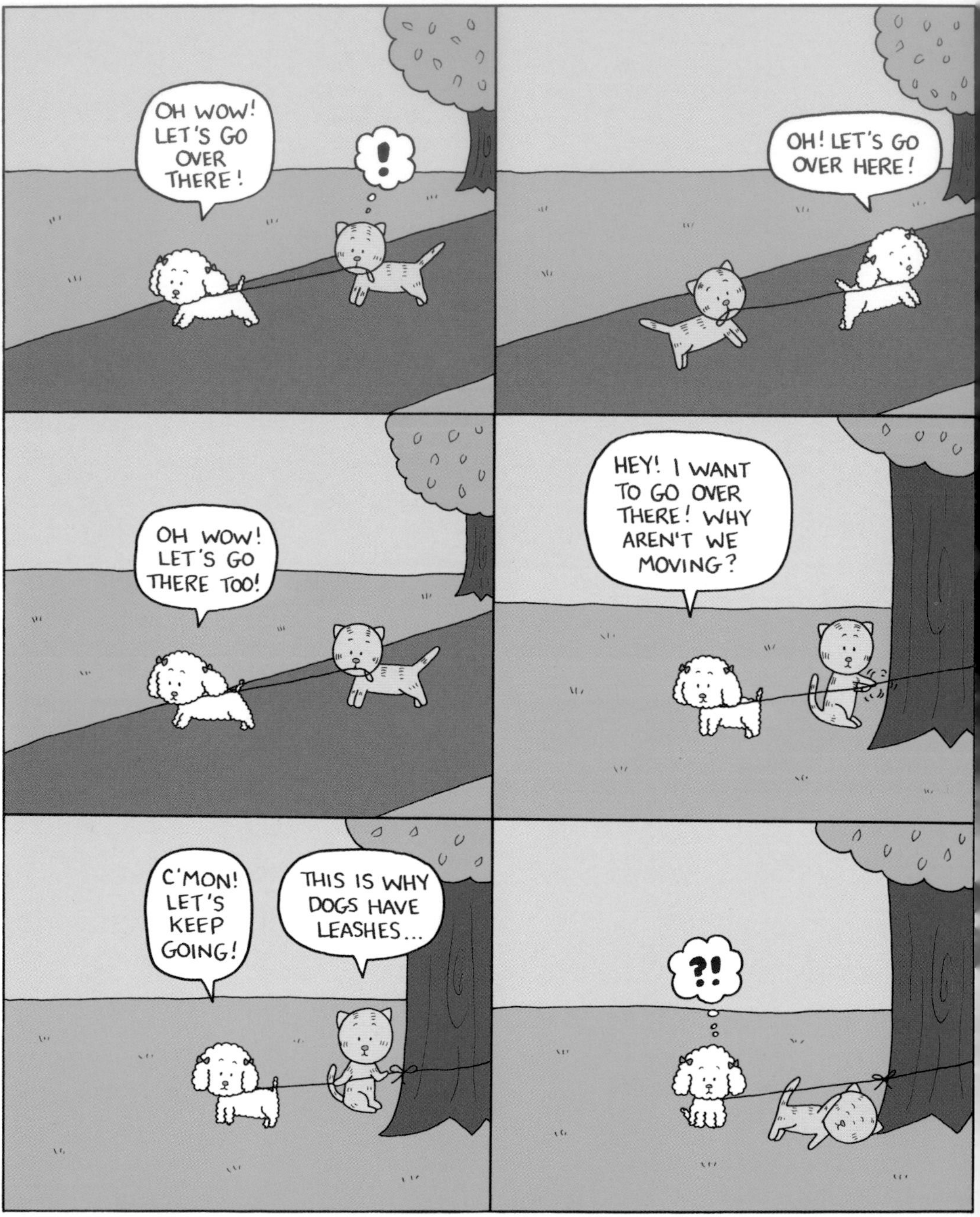
OH WOW! LET'S GO OVER THERE!
!
OH! LET'S GO OVER HERE!
OH WOW! LET'S GO THERE TOO!
HEY! I WANT TO GO OVER THERE! WHY AREN'T WE MOVING?
C'MON! LET'S KEEP GOING!
THIS IS WHY DOGS HAVE LEASHES...
?!

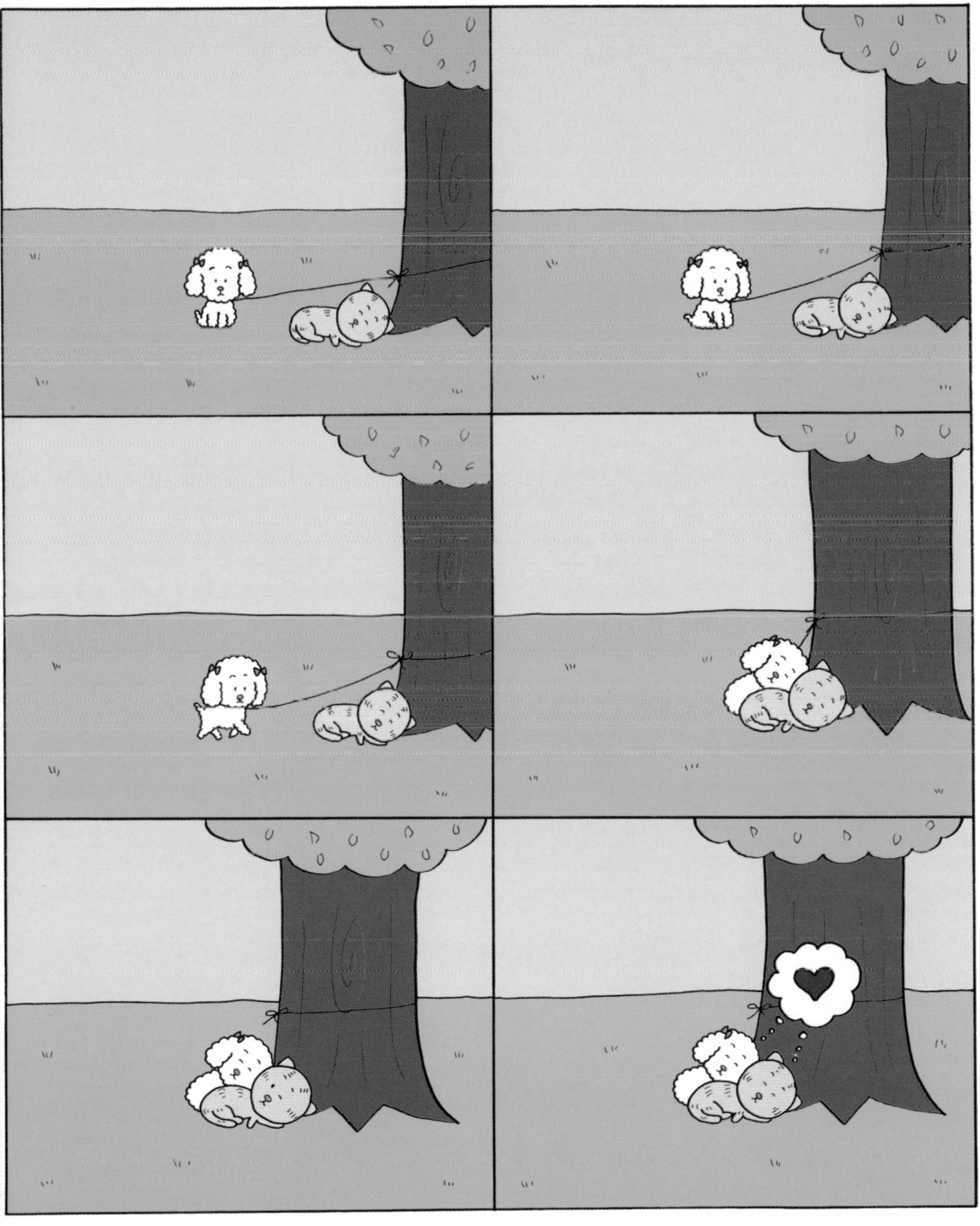

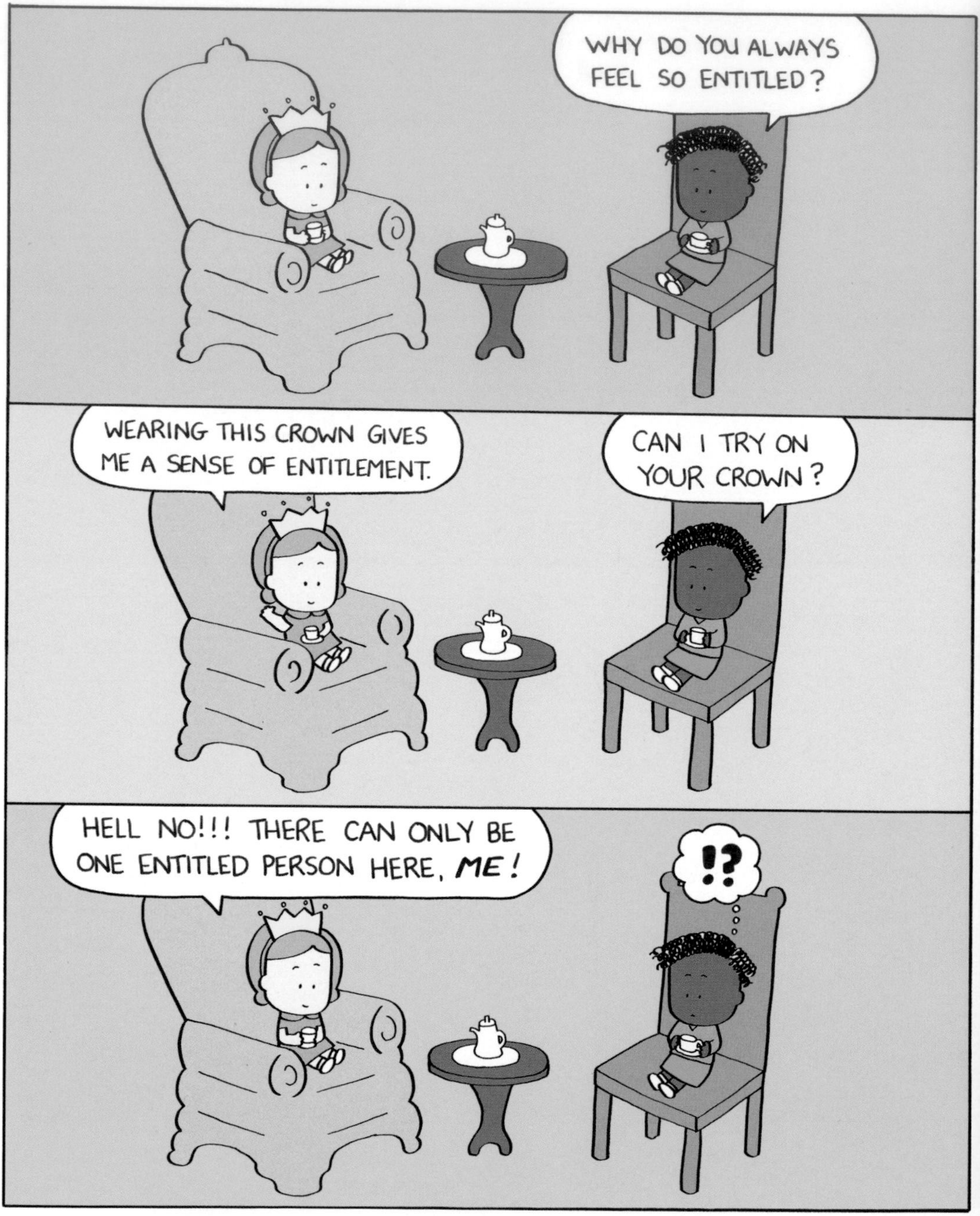
WHY DO YOU ALWAYS FEEL SO ENTITLED?
WEARING THIS CROWN GIVES ME A SENSE OF ENTITLEMENT.
CAN I TRY ON YOUR CROWN?
HELL NO!!! THERE CAN ONLY BE ONE ENTITLED PERSON HERE, *ME*!
!?

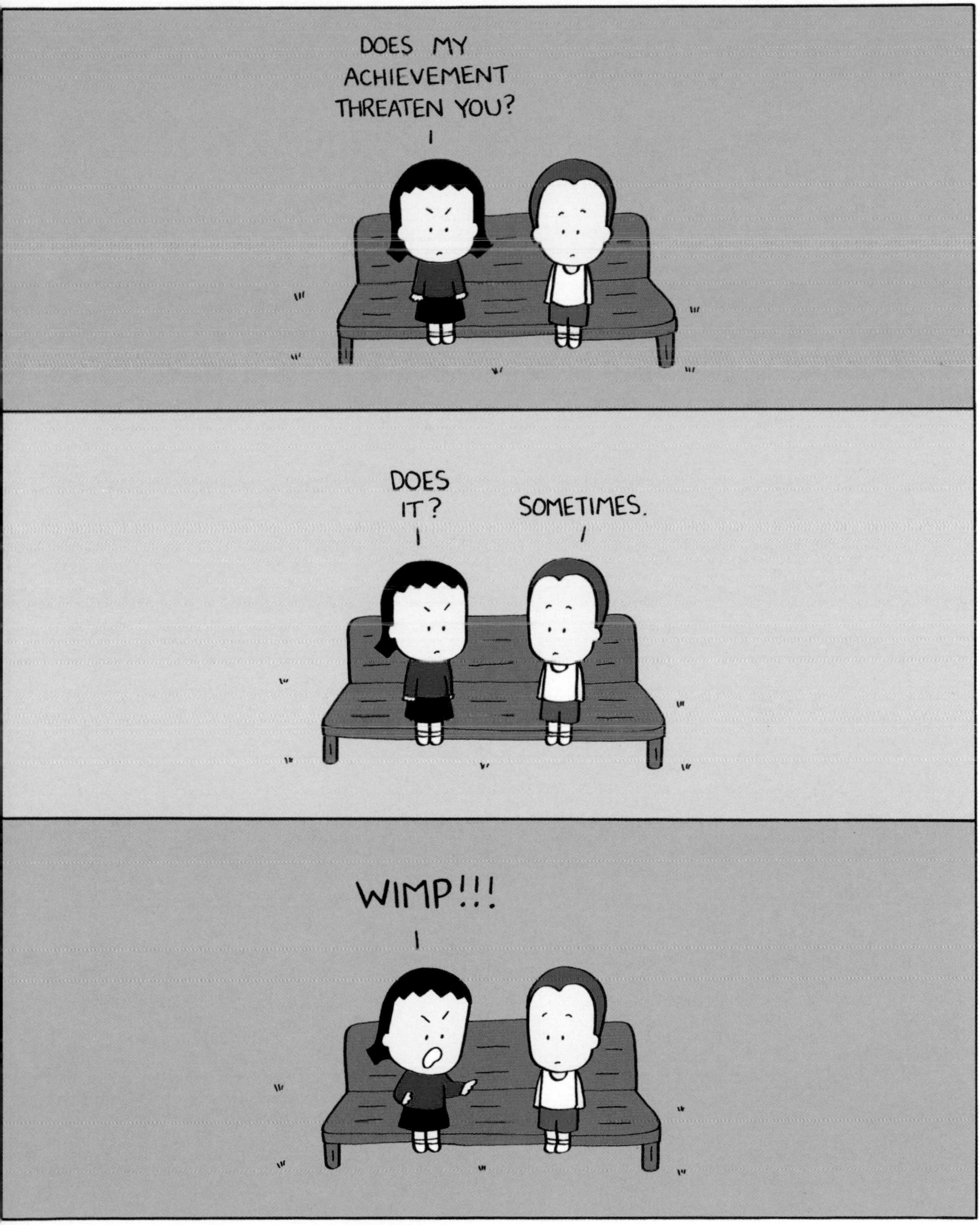
DOES MY ACHIEVEMENT THREATEN YOU?
DOES IT?
SOMETIMES.
WIMP!!!

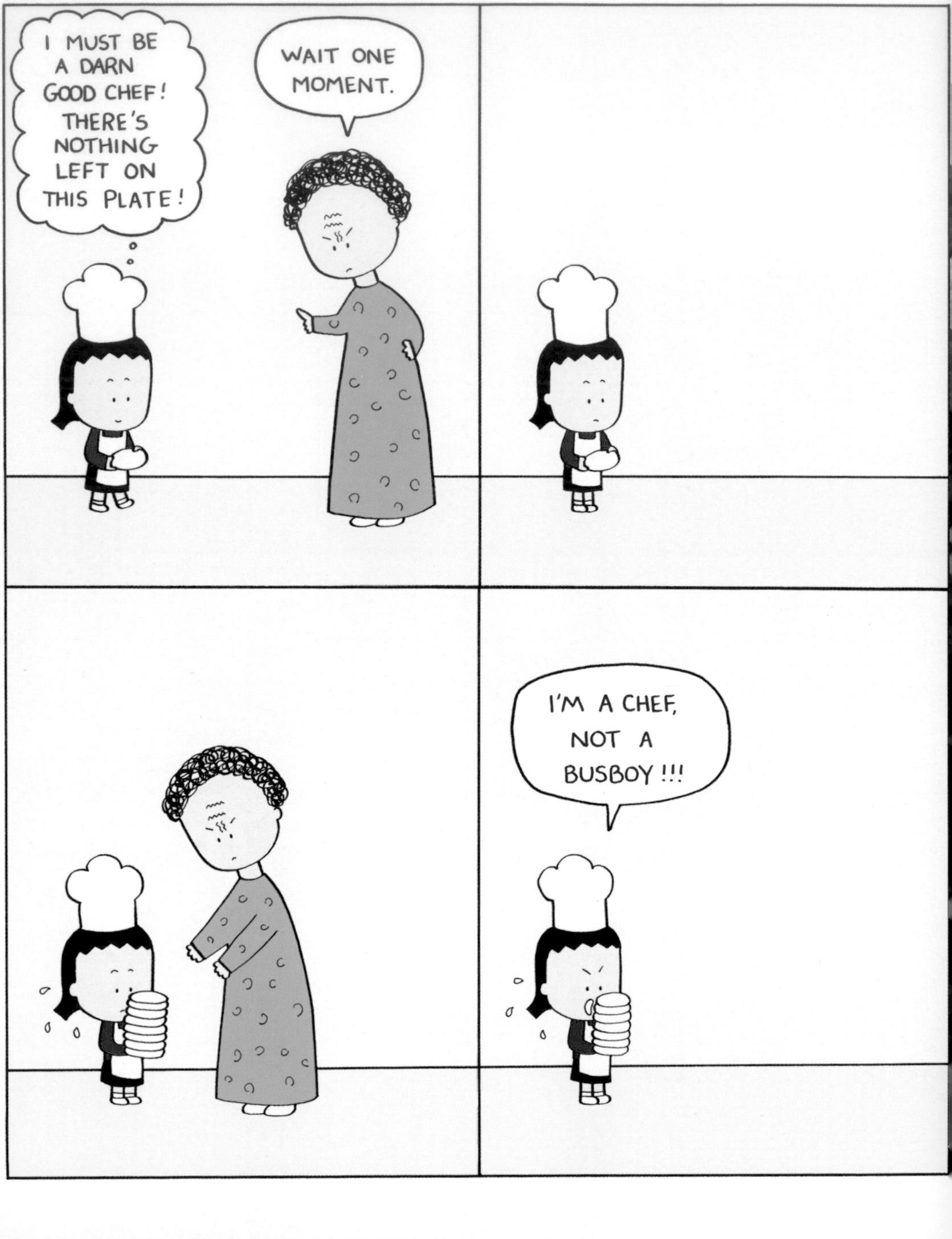
I MUST BE A DARN GOOD CHEF! THERE'S NOTHING LEFT ON THIS PLATE!
WAIT ONE MOMENT.
I'M A CHEF, NOT A BUSBOY!!!

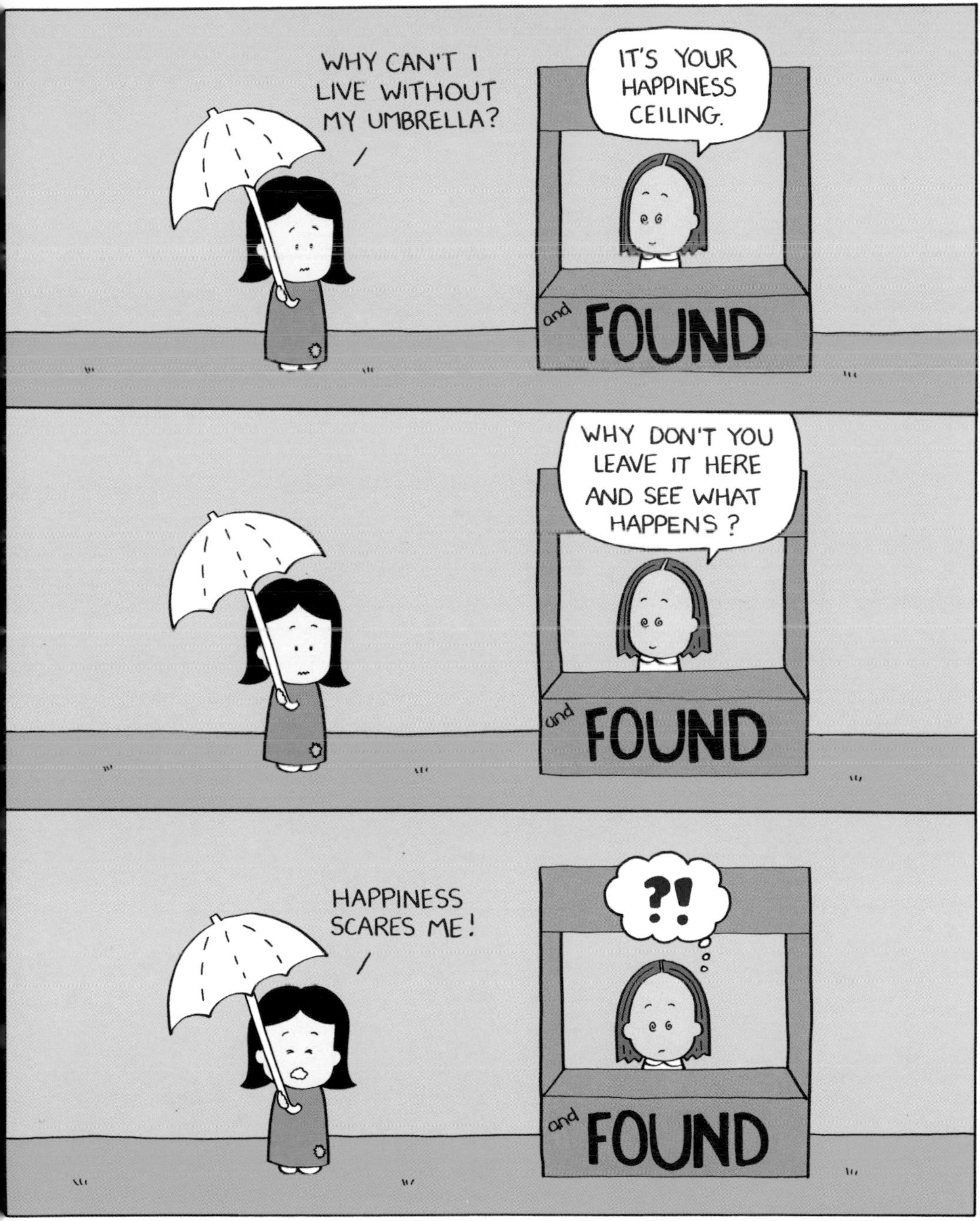
WHY CAN'T I LIVE WITHOUT MY UMBRELLA?
IT'S YOUR HAPPINESS CEILING.
and FOUND
WHY DON'T YOU LEAVE IT HERE AND SEE WHAT HAPPENS?
and FOUND
HAPPINESS SCARES ME!
?!
and FOUND

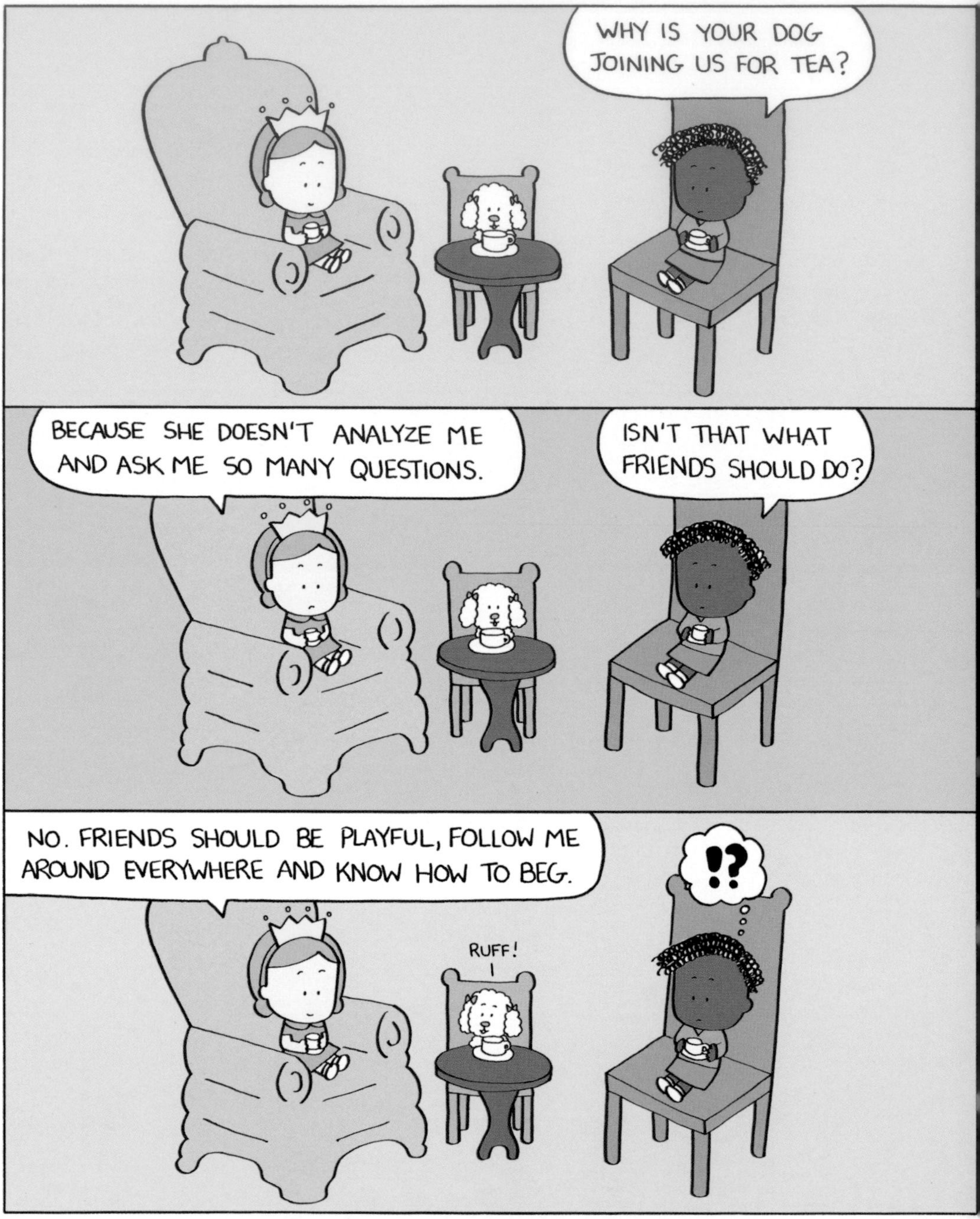
WHY IS YOUR DOG JOINING US FOR TEA?
BECAUSE SHE DOESN'T ANALYZE ME AND ASK ME SO MANY QUESTIONS.
ISN'T THAT WHAT FRIENDS SHOULD DO?
NO. FRIENDS SHOULD BE PLAYFUL, FOLLOW ME AROUND EVERYWHERE AND KNOW HOW TO BEG.
RUFF!
!?

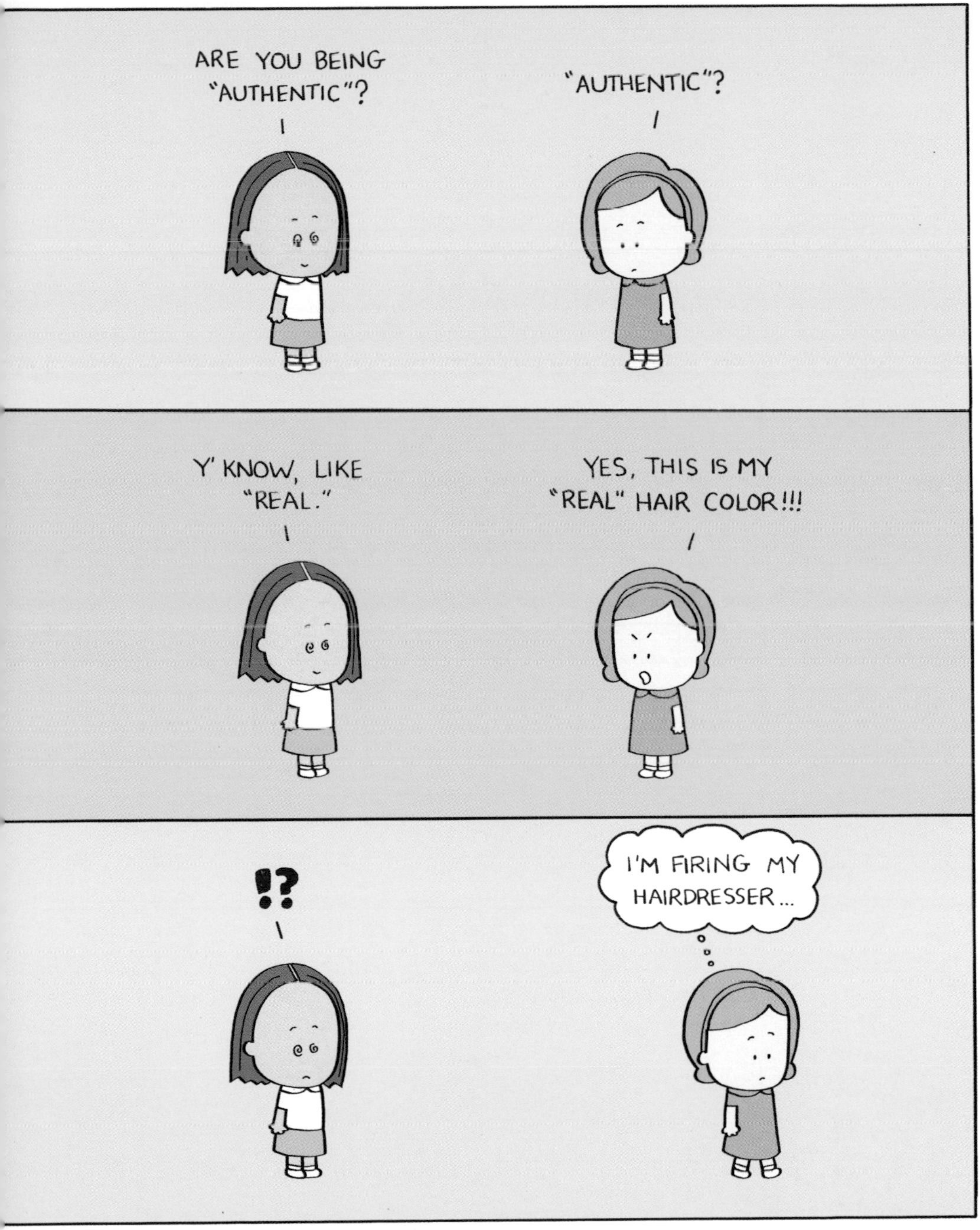
ARE YOU BEING "AUTHENTIC"?
"AUTHENTIC"?
Y' KNOW, LIKE "REAL."
YES, THIS IS MY "REAL" HAIR COLOR!!!
!?
I'M FIRING MY HAIRDRESSER...

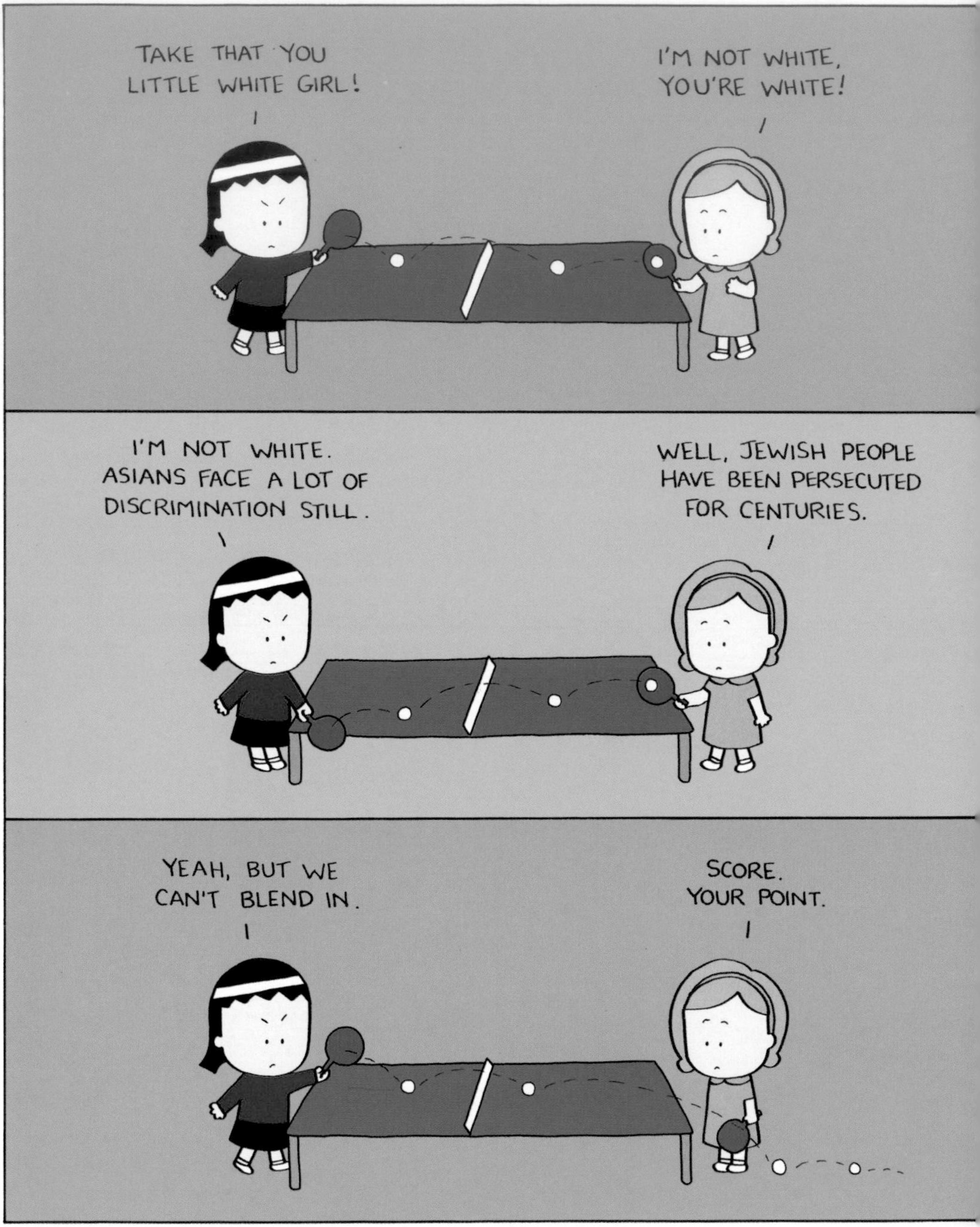
TAKE THAT YOU LITTLE WHITE GIRL!
I'M NOT WHITE, YOU'RE WHITE!
I'M NOT WHITE. ASIANS FACE A LOT OF DISCRIMINATION STILL.
WELL, JEWISH PEOPLE HAVE BEEN PERSECUTED FOR CENTURIES.
YEAH, BUT WE CAN'T BLEND IN.
SCORE. YOUR POINT.

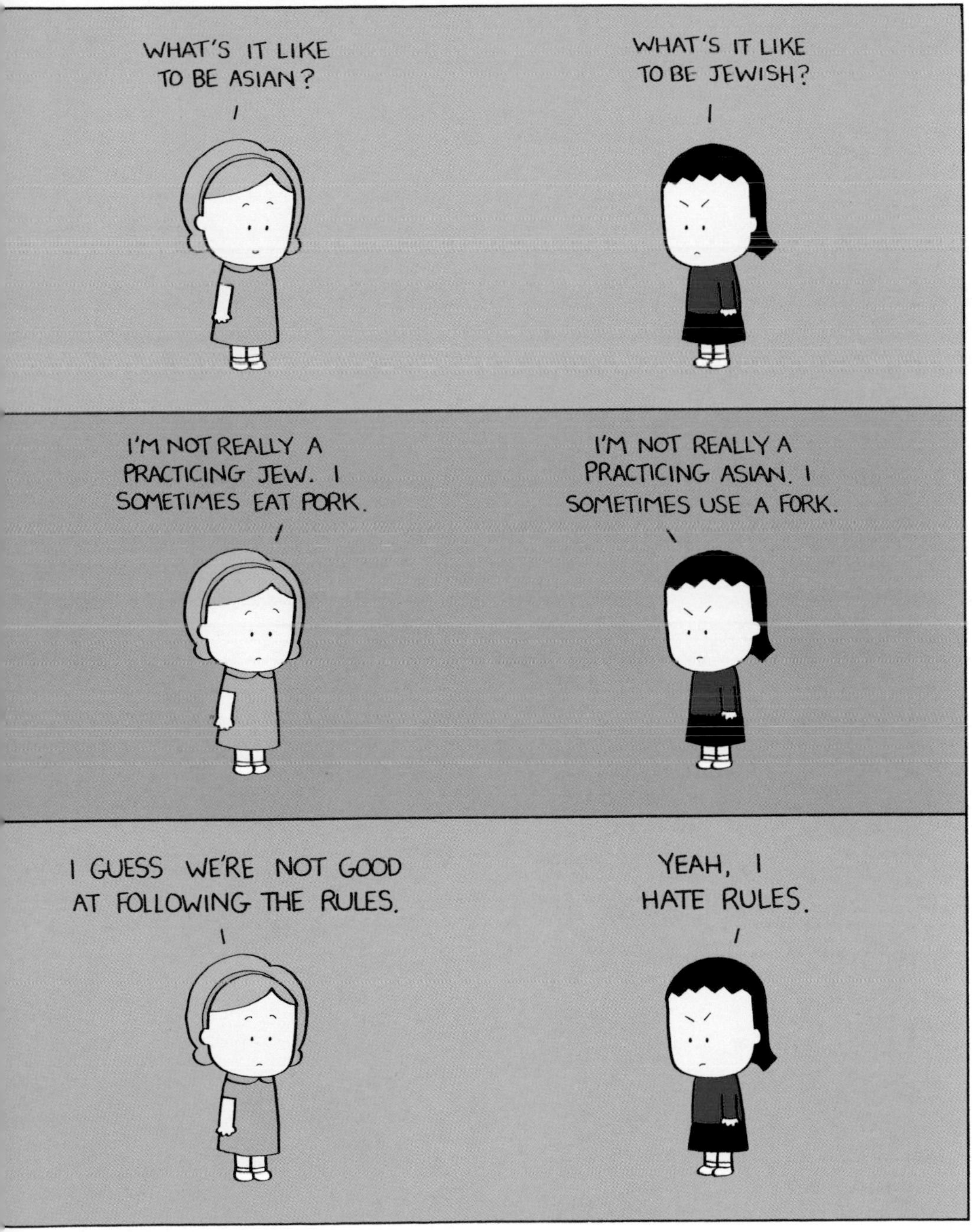
WHAT'S IT LIKE TO BE ASIAN?
WHAT'S IT LIKE TO BE JEWISH?
I'M NOT REALLY A PRACTICING JEW. I SOMETIMES EAT PORK.
I'M NOT REALLY A PRACTICING ASIAN. I SOMETIMES USE A FORK.
I GUESS WE'RE NOT GOOD AT FOLLOWING THE RULES.
YEAH, I HATE RULES.

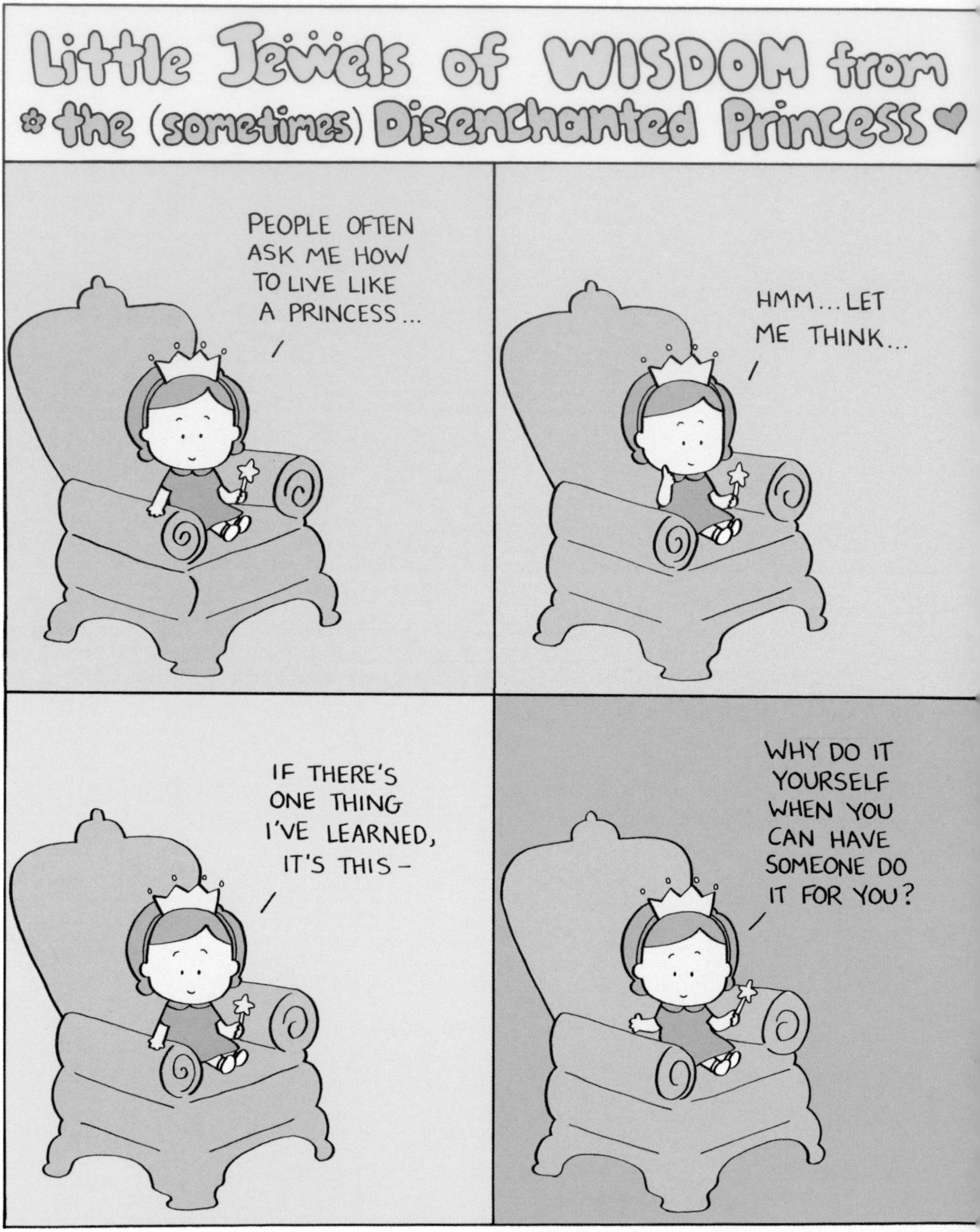
Little Jewels of WISDOM from the (sometimes) Disenchanted Princess
PEOPLE OFTEN ASK ME HOW TO LIVE LIKE A PRINCESS...
HMM... LET ME THINK...
IF THERE'S ONE THING I'VE LEARNED, IT'S THIS –
WHY DO IT YOURSELF WHEN YOU CAN HAVE SOMEONE DO IT FOR YOU?

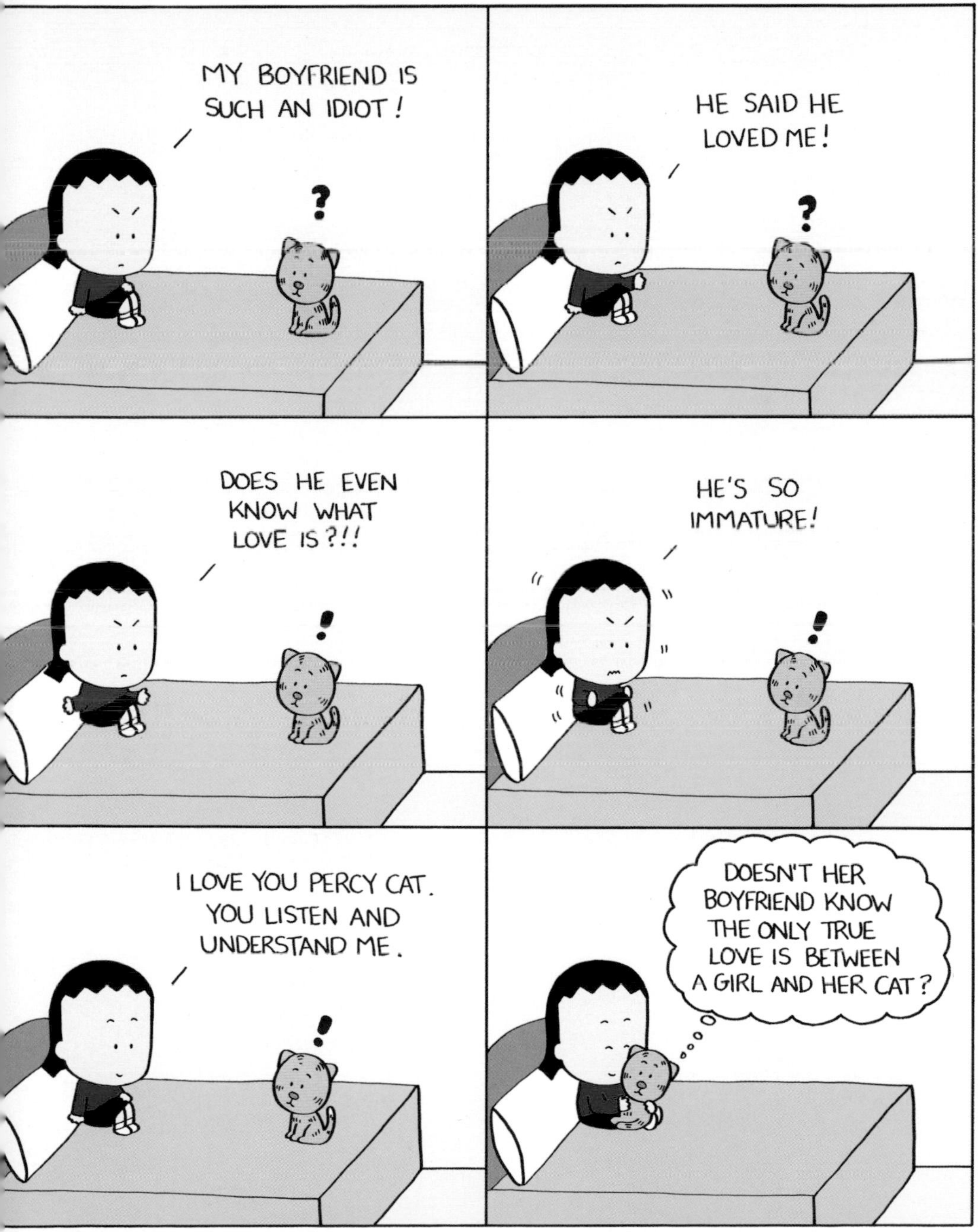
MY BOYFRIEND IS SUCH AN IDIOT!
?
HE SAID HE LOVED ME!
?
DOES HE EVEN KNOW WHAT LOVE IS?!!
!
HE'S SO IMMATURE!
!
I LOVE YOU PERCY CAT. YOU LISTEN AND UNDERSTAND ME.
!
DOESN'T HER BOYFRIEND KNOW THE ONLY TRUE LOVE IS BETWEEN A GIRL AND HER CAT?

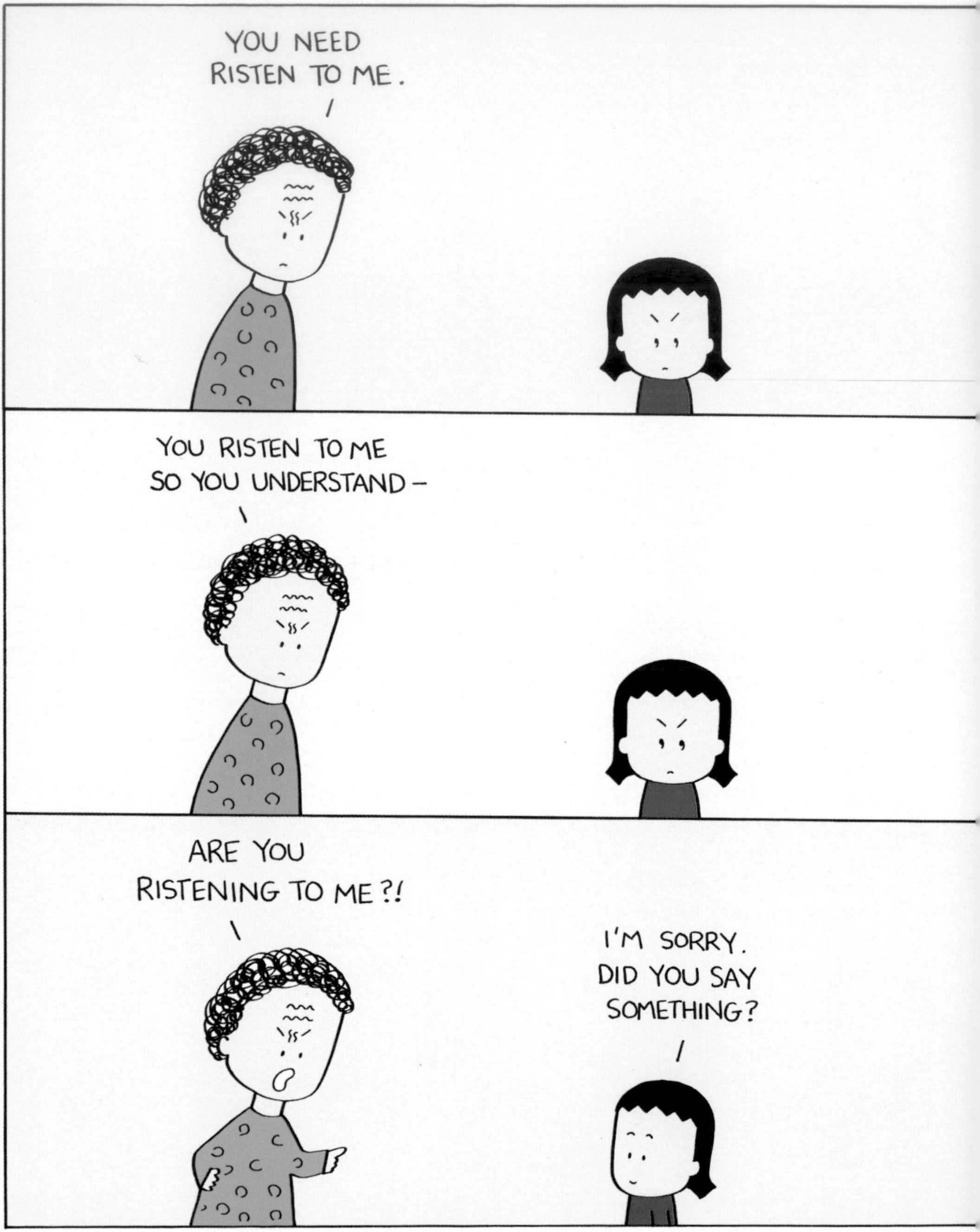
YOU NEED RISTEN TO ME.
YOU RISTEN TO ME SO YOU UNDERSTAND–
ARE YOU RISTENING TO ME?!
I'M SORRY. DID YOU SAY SOMETHING?

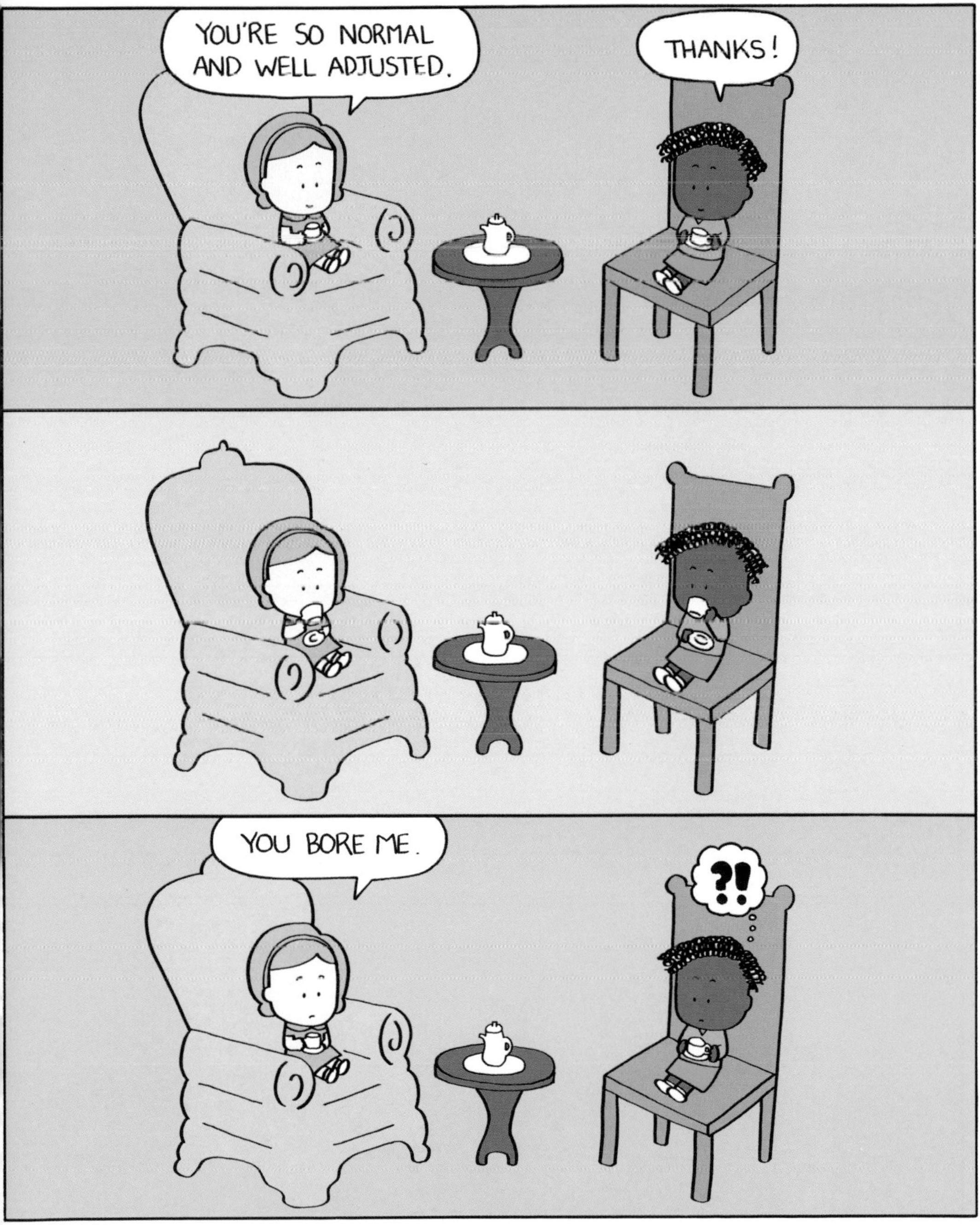
YOU'RE SO NORMAL AND WELL ADJUSTED.
THANKS!
YOU BORE ME.
?!

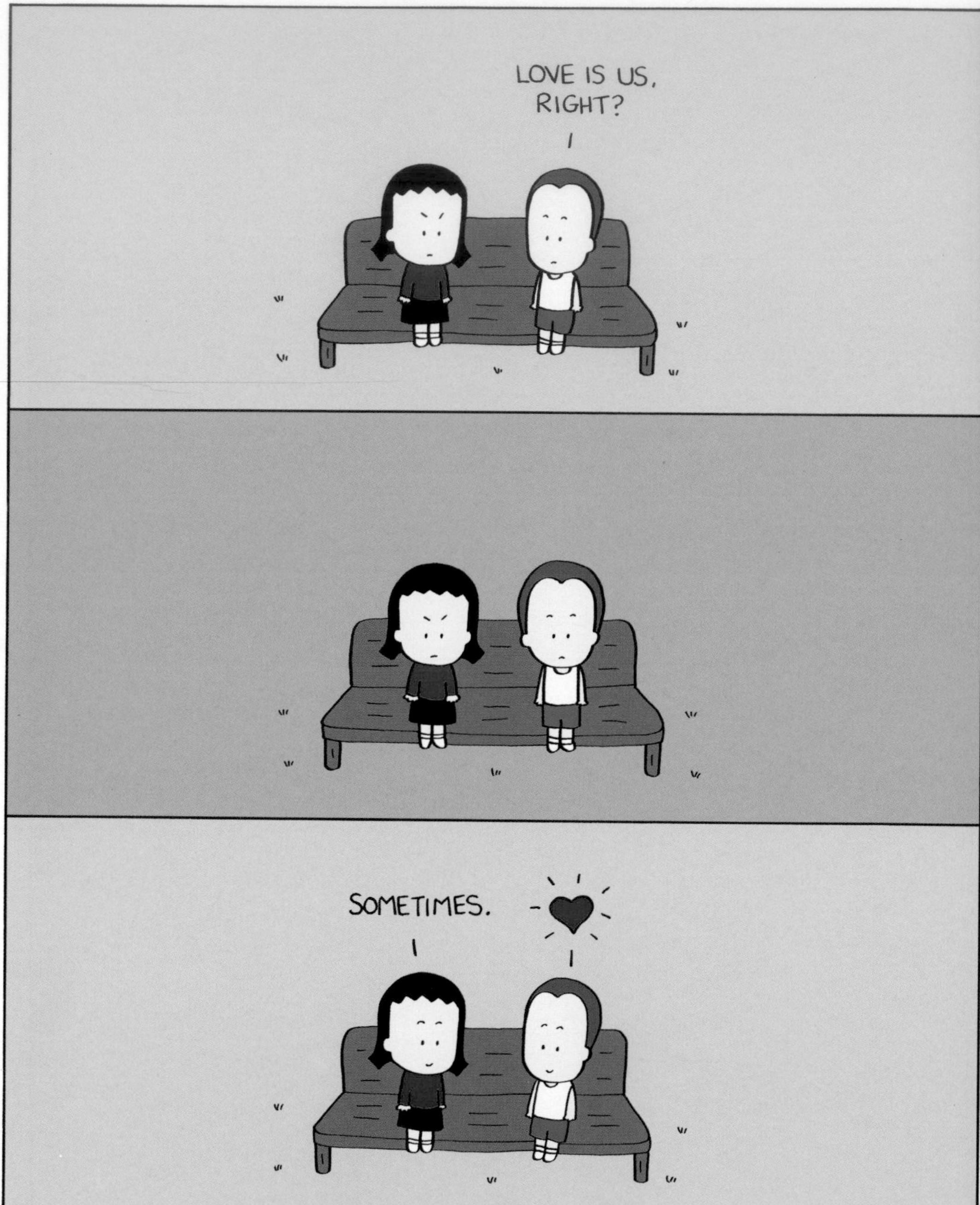
LOVE IS US, RIGHT?
SOMETIMES.

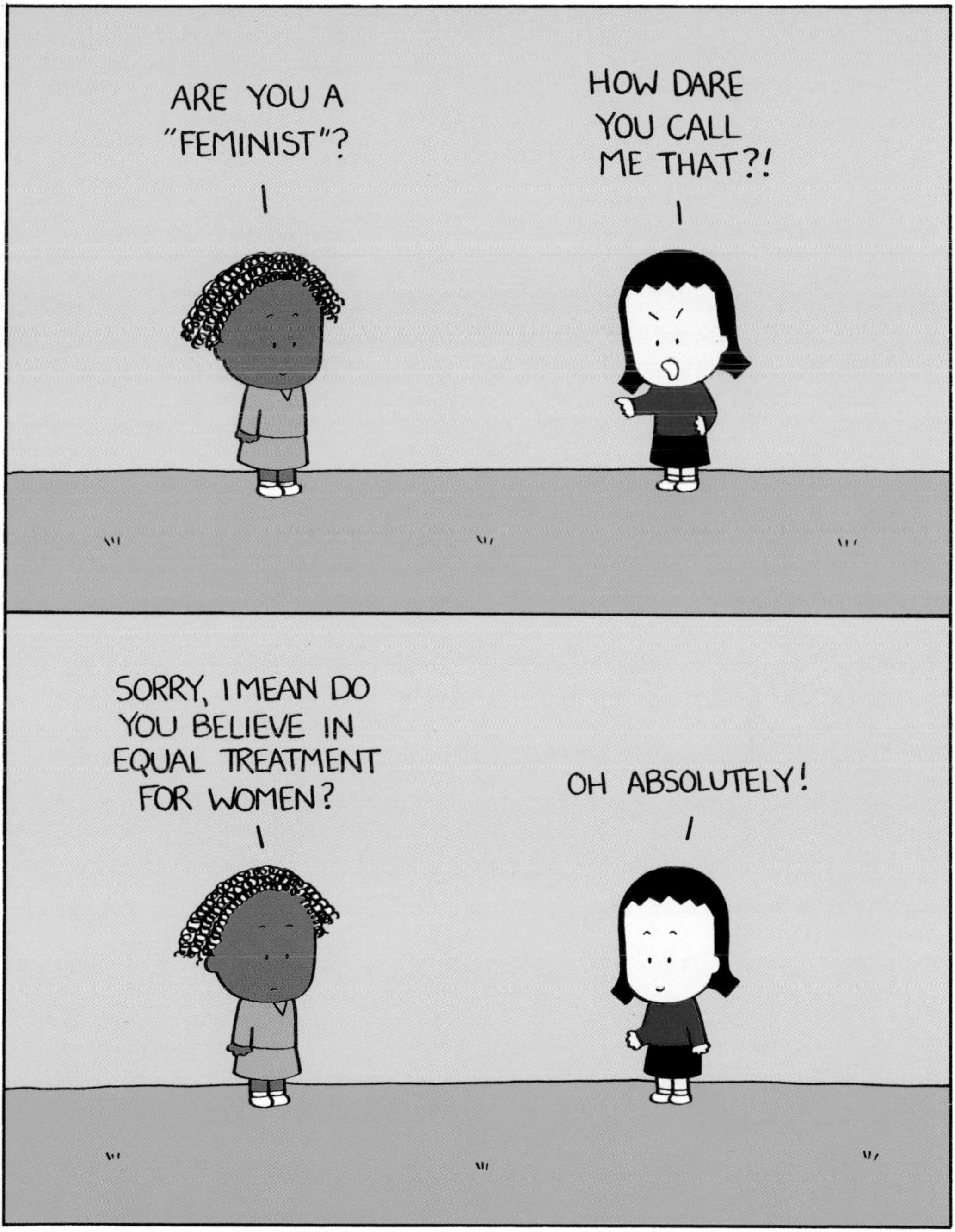
ARE YOU A "FEMINIST"?
HOW DARE YOU CALL ME THAT?!
SORRY, I MEAN DO YOU BELIEVE IN EQUAL TREATMENT FOR WOMEN?
OH ABSOLUTELY!

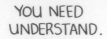
YOU NEED
UNDERSTAND.

UNDERSTAND
WHAT?

YOU NEED UNDERSTAND
MY COUNTRY.

YOU MEAN
AMERICA?

NO, WHERE WE FROM
ORIGINAL, MOTHER COUNTRY.

WHY? SO THAT
MOTHER CAN
NAG ME TOO?

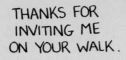
THANKS FOR
INVITING ME
ON YOUR WALK.

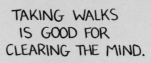
TAKING WALKS
IS GOOD FOR
CLEARING THE MIND.

SORRY, I CAN'T WALK
WITH YOU ANYMORE.
I WORKED HARD TO
GET THE THOUGHTS
I HAVE IN MY HEAD.

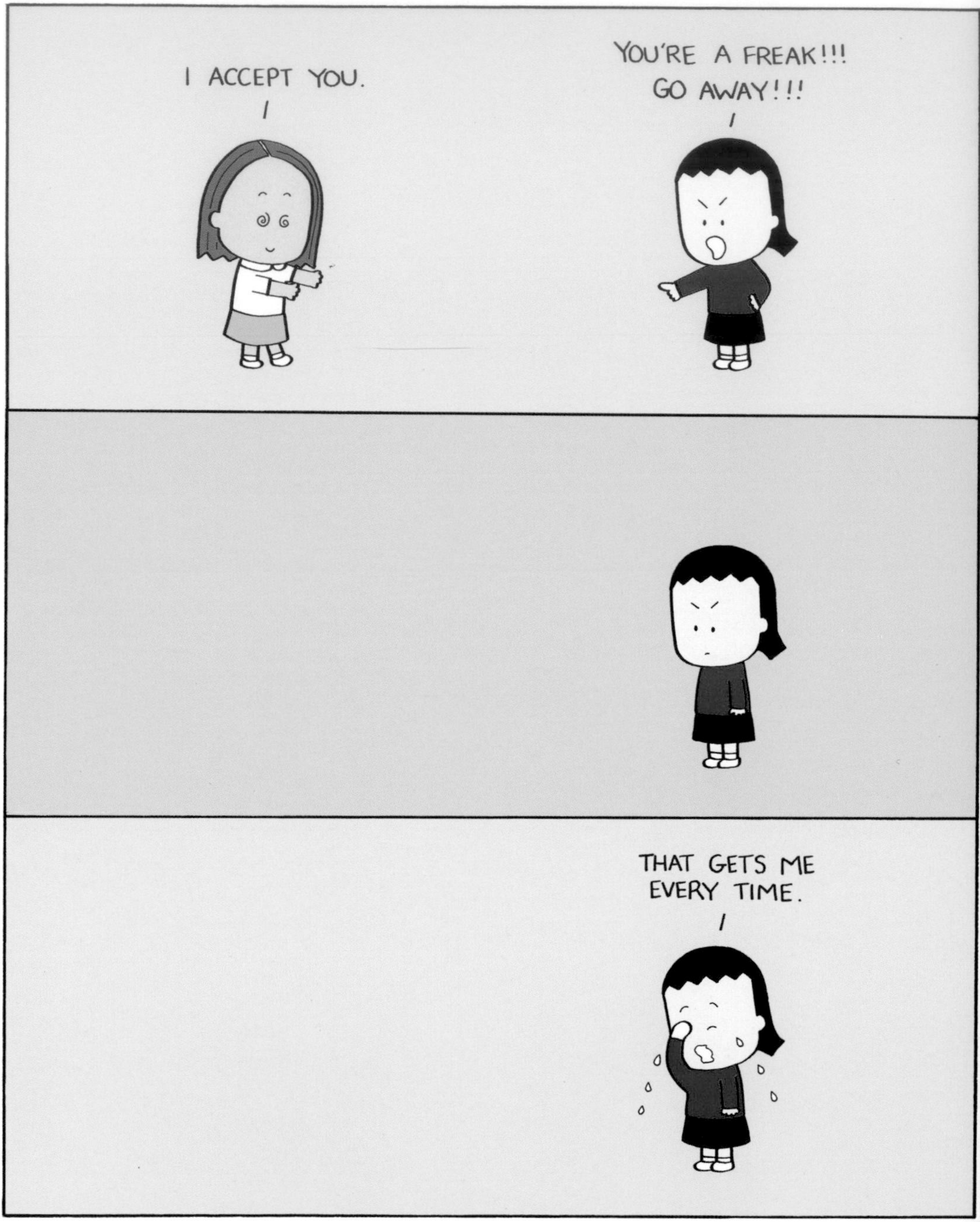
I ACCEPT YOU.
YOU'RE A FREAK!!! GO AWAY!!!
THAT GETS ME EVERY TIME.

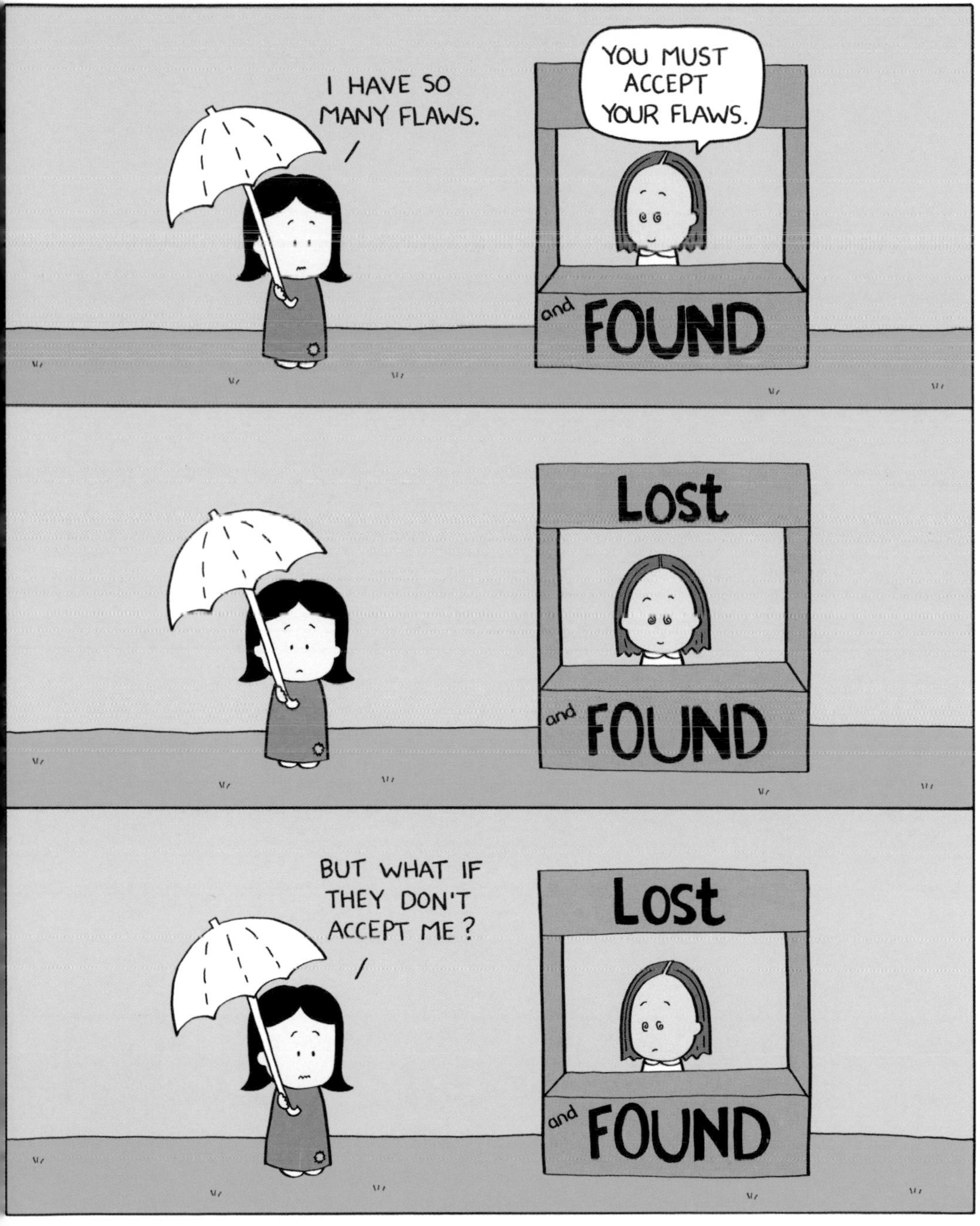
I HAVE SO MANY FLAWS.
YOU MUST ACCEPT YOUR FLAWS.
and FOUND
Lost
and FOUND
BUT WHAT IF THEY DON'T ACCEPT ME?
Lost
and FOUND

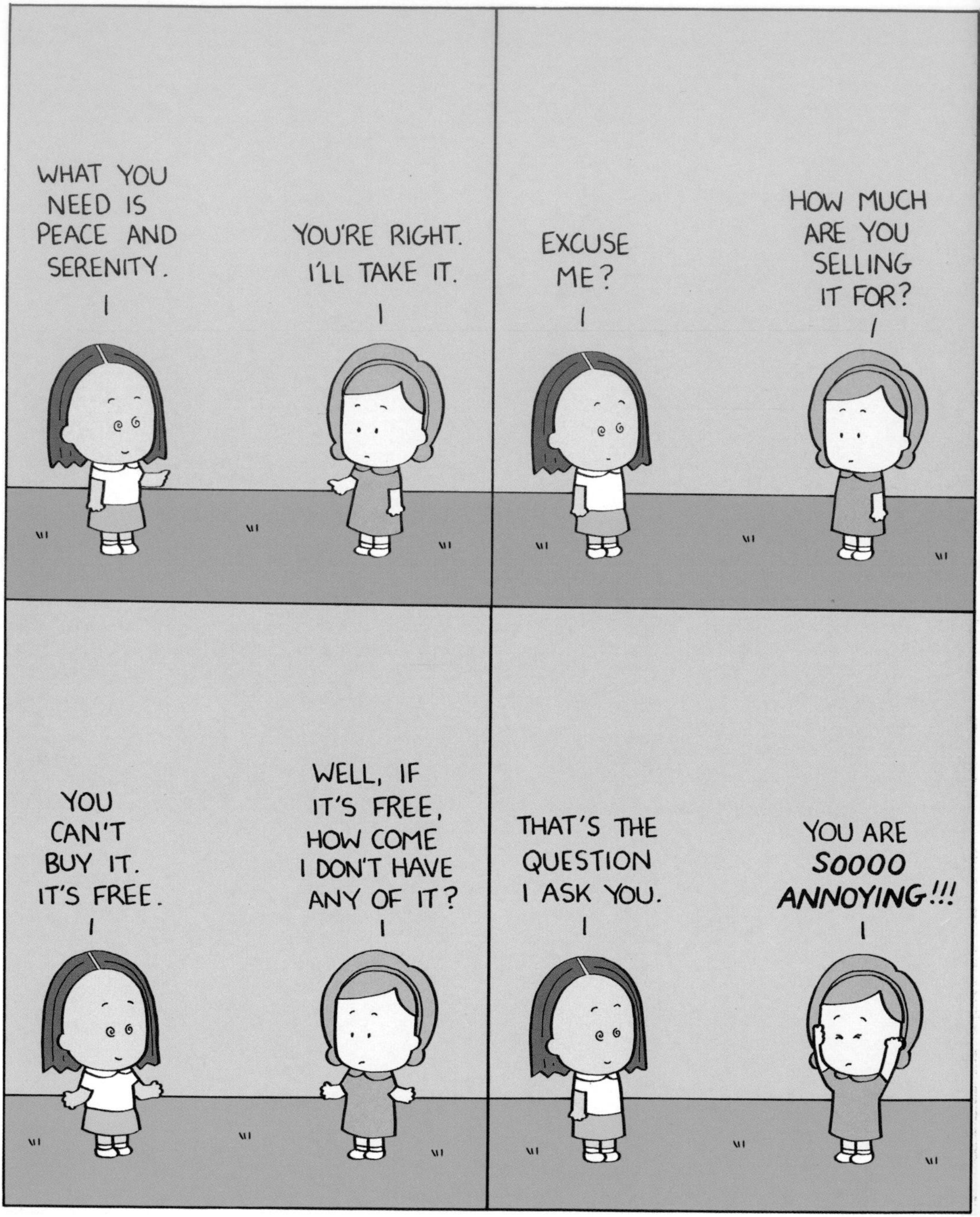
WHAT YOU NEED IS PEACE AND SERENITY.
YOU'RE RIGHT. I'LL TAKE IT.
EXCUSE ME?
HOW MUCH ARE YOU SELLING IT FOR?
YOU CAN'T BUY IT. IT'S FREE.
WELL, IF IT'S FREE, HOW COME I DON'T HAVE ANY OF IT?
THAT'S THE QUESTION I ASK YOU.
YOU ARE SOOOO ANNOYING!!!

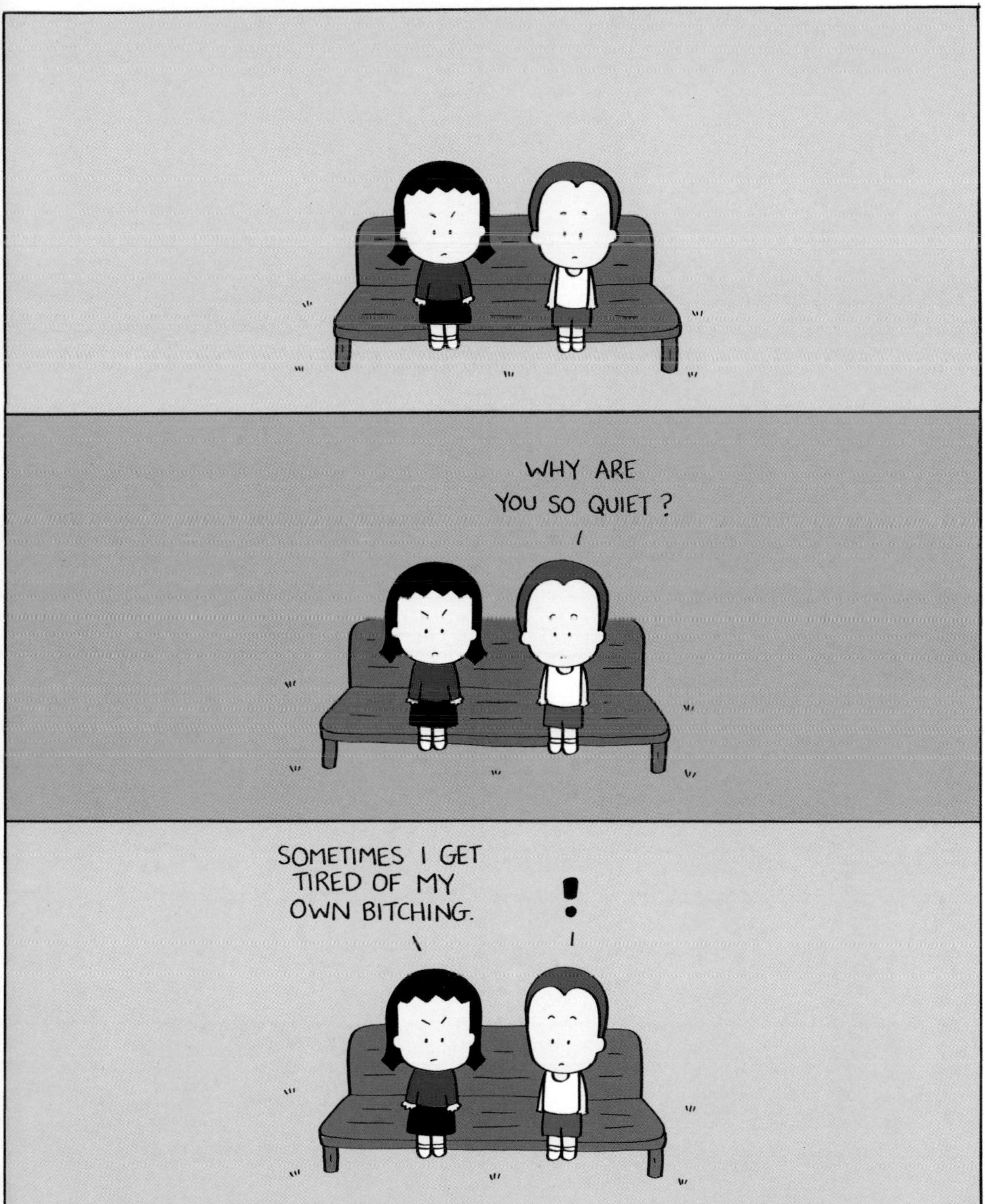
WHY ARE YOU SO QUIET?
SOMETIMES I GET TIRED OF MY OWN BITCHING.
!

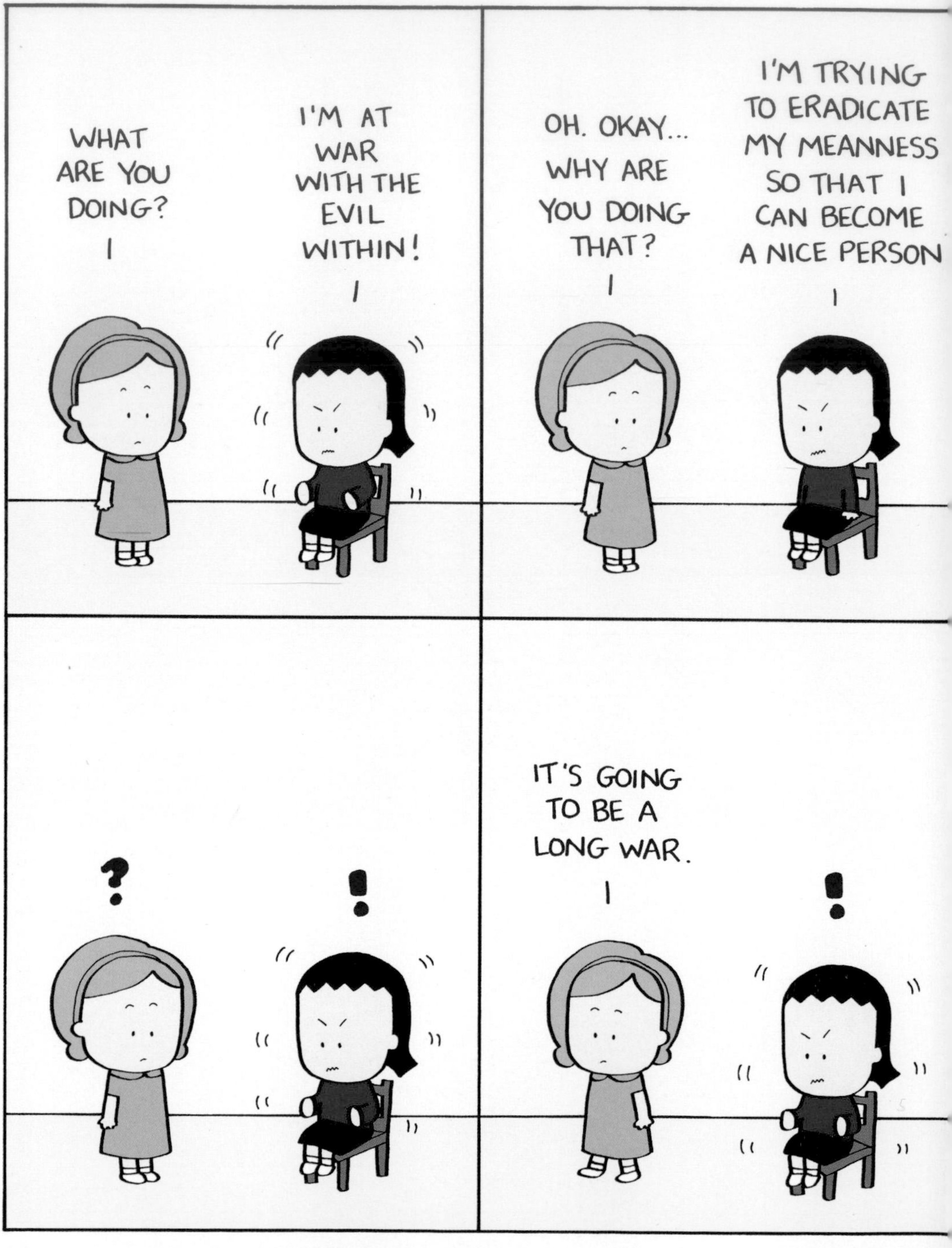
WHAT ARE YOU DOING?
I'M AT WAR WITH THE EVIL WITHIN!
OH. OKAY... WHY ARE YOU DOING THAT?
I'M TRYING TO ERADICATE MY MEANNESS SO THAT I CAN BECOME A NICE PERSON
?
!
IT'S GOING TO BE A LONG WAR.
!

The Angry Little Girls Guide to Moods

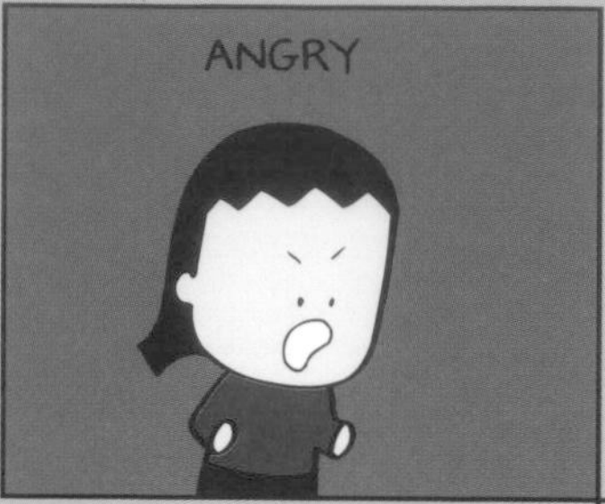
ANGRY

Here is the angry little Asian girl, Kim. This is her usual mood, ANGRY!

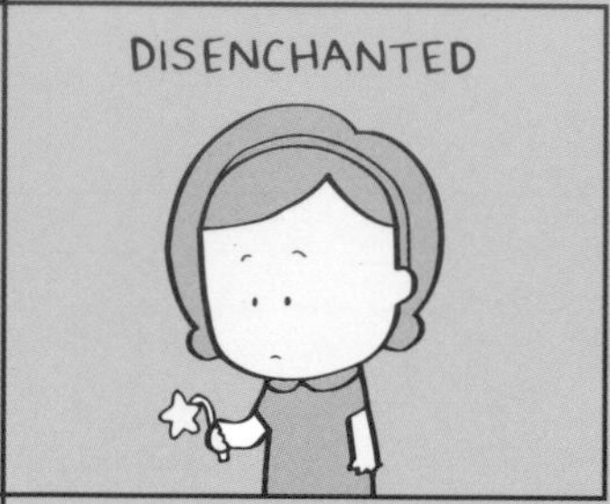
DISENCHANTED

The disenchanted princess, Deborah. She's a princess who has it all, but she's still not happy! She's so DISENCHANTED.

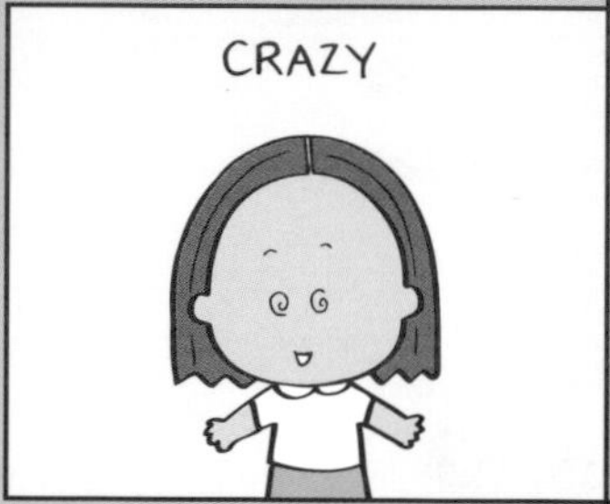
CRAZY

The crazy little Latina, Maria. She can see and feel the things that normal people don't take the time to notice. So is she really CRAZY?

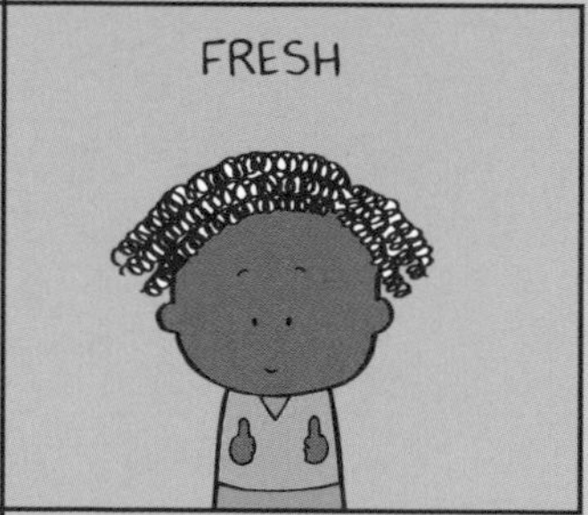
FRESH

The fresh little soul sistah, Wanda. She's always in a good mood. She's FRESH!

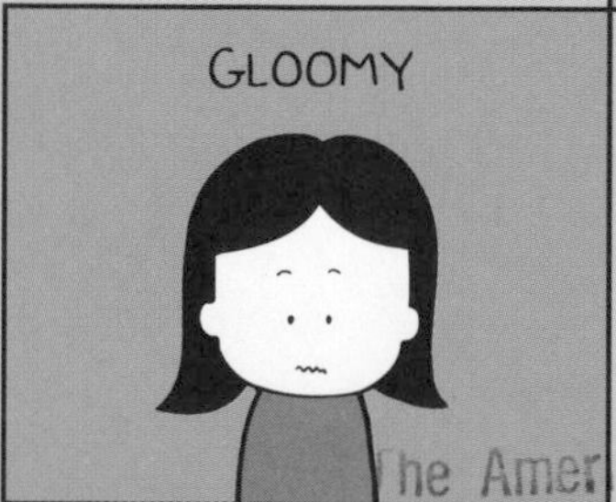
GLOOMY

The gloomy girl, Xyla. She sees doom and danger everywhere. She's so GLOOMY!